SPECIAL PRAISE FOR

We Regret to Inform You

★

"*We Regret to Inform You* helps fill the void in grief resources on military loss for surviving parents of our fallen service members. Parents will find not only reliable guidance for coping with the life-changing loss of their son or daughter in military service, but also the validation that their child's service to country mattered, is deeply appreciated, and will not be forgotten. All who served and died because of that service will be remembered."

General Glenn M. Walters
US Marine Corps (Ret)

"Even fifteen years after my son was killed, I found the book resonated with me and shed new light on surviving, adjusting, and moving forward after his death.

We Regret to Inform You is the only book of its kind for bereaved parents of military service members, providing us with information about the military and grieving process, and illuminating for us the path of our journey. It is well researched and written, thorough in scope, organized for easy use, and written in language that is readily understood.

Betsy Beard
Gold Star Mother of SPC Bradley Beard, US Army
Editor, TAPS Magazine (2008-2015)

"Joanne Steen offers us a glimpse of how life changes suddenly, permanently, and immeasurably when parents lose a child in the service of their country. From the vantage point of her own personal grief, Joanne tells a powerful story that deserves to be told about sacrifice that needs to be understood."

General Martin E. Dempsey
US Army (Ret)

"After our son was killed while serving in Pakistan, I searched for books on the loss of a child. Many focused on losing a young child, some focused on losing your child to suicide, but there were none that dealt with the military death of one's son or daughter. After reading several of those books, I still felt like there were pieces of my grief puzzle that were missing. This book put into words and validated those missing pieces. It helped my husband and me to understand the unique circumstances of a military death. And that we not only lost our son but also our connection with the military community, with the soldiers who were his 'brothers' and 'sisters' in arms. Joanne's clear descriptions helped me to put into words and understand the emotions I was feeling.

All in all, *We Regret To Inform You* supplied the answers and understanding that those other grief books did not have. Thank you Joanne!"

Nancy Stets
Proud Gold Star Mom of SSG Mark A. Stets Jr, US Army

"I wish I had this book soon after my military son, US Marine Sgt. Thomas R. Bagosy completed suicide. Tommy was my second son, age twenty-five, a combat veteran of two deployments to Iraq 2006/07 and Afghanistan 2009. He died on May 10, 2010 while on active duty at Camp Lejeune, NC.

Every word in *We Regret to Inform You* applies to the grief experienced by my family and me. The Tips for Surviving Fathers was especially helpful in that men have to contend with years of ingrained conditioning for dealing with grief. We have been conditioned to not show emotion or cry. I only wish I had the details of what to expect that I found in this book."

Bob Bagosy

Proud Gold Star Father of Sgt. Thomas R. Bagosy, US Marine Corps
Semper Fi Tommy!

"Joanne Steen's *We Regret to Inform You* is a consoling gift and a compassionate guide to Gold Star families surviving the loss of a child in a military setting. Families will find useful information and support as they begin their journey with grief."

Kenneth J. Doka, PhD

Professor, the Graduate School of The College of New Rochelle
Senior Consultant, the Hospice Foundation of America

"*We Regret To Inform You* is a comprehensive, yet practical guide to understanding and coping with losing a son or daughter in military service. Whether you are a parent grieving your child's death, a caring friend, or a professional counselor this book will prove an invaluable resource in navigating the complexities of this unimaginable journey."

George Lutz

Gold Star Father of Cpl. George "Tony" Lutz, US Army
Founder of Honor and Remember, Inc.

"Of all the books I've recommended to others on grief, this is one of the best. Ms. Steen artfully weaves her knowledge of grief into each chapter in a way that helps Gold Star parents feel understood and validated. *We Regret to Inform You* is an important contribution that poignantly steps the reader through all aspects of the grief journey, providing hope and promise for better days. Steen quotes a number of bereaved parents throughout the book in a way that is compassionate and at the same time pragmatic. Explaining what to expect and how to respond to the challenges of military loss, this book is not only for those who are bereaved but for anyone supporting this type of loss."

Patti Anewalt, PhD, LPC, FT
Director of Pathways Center for Grief & Loss
Hospice & Community Care

"In my more than thirty years as a grief counselor, author, and educator, I have learned there is a profound need for compassionate and focused care provided to Gold Star parents. A military widow herself, Joanne Steen brings her incredible empathy and intelligence to these pages and helps fill this need. *We Regret to Inform You* weaves together real voices and practical guidance, and is a necessary read for those affected as well as their family, friends, and professional caregivers."

Alan Wolfelt, PhD, CT
Center for Loss and Life Transition

"*We Regret to Inform You* is one of the best books I've seen to date to assist Gold Star parents in grappling with the pain of the loss of their daughter or son. Joanne's writing style is the same as being with her in person: compassionate, warm, and engaging. The book has numerous quotes from Gold Star parents interspersed throughout it to let them know that however they lost their child— regardless of age, whether in combat, a training accident, a reserve drill weekend activity, or suicide—they are not alone. I strongly recommend this book as a guide for the parents and also as a 'quick reach' reference book for military chaplains and civilian clergy who walk the hard path of being with a Gold Star parent."[*]

Fr. William D. Razz Waff, DMin, BCC
Major General, US Army (Ret)
Executive Director, Military Chaplains Association

[*]The above comments do not represent an endorsement by the Department of Defense, the Department of the Army, or the Military Chaplains Association.

"As a former Chief of Naval Personnel who had the honor and challenge of leading the Navy's team supporting families whose service member was killed in the terrorist attacks on the USS Cole in 2000 and the 9/11 attack on the Pentagon, I wish I'd been able to share Joanne Steen's remarkable book *We Regret To Inform You* with not only my team, but also the parents of all who were killed. Quite simply, I know of no one more knowledgeable than Ms. Steen on how to help parents, spouses, and family members work through the traumatic loss of their service member. This is a must have book for all in key leadership positions, too."

Vice Admiral Norbert Ryan
US Navy (Ret)

"This book is a wonderful resource for parents grieving the death of their child who served in the military. Joanne compassionately covers the impact that military deaths have on parents and normalizes grief as a prolonged journey. She provides insight on first surviving the death of an adult child and then eventually moving forward in a healthy way."

Gregory Inman, PhD
Clinical psychologist

We Regret to Inform You

Joanne Steen

WE REGRET TO INFORM YOU

A Survival Guide for
GOLD STAR PARENTS
and Those Who Support Them

CRP
CENTRAL RECOVERY PRESS

Las Vegas

Central Recovery Press (CRP) is committed to publishing exceptional materials addressing addiction treatment, recovery, and behavioral healthcare topics.

For more information, visit www.centralrecoverypress.com.

Publisher: Central Recovery Press
            3321 N. Buffalo Drive
            Las Vegas, NV 89129

24 23 22 21 20 19   1 2 3 4 5

Library of Congress Cataloging-in-Publication Data

Names: Steen, Joanne M., author.
Title: We regret to inform you : a survival guide for Gold Star parents /
   Joanne Steen.
Other titles: Survival guide for Gold Star parents
Description: Las Vegas : Central Recovery Press, 2019. | Includes
   bibliographical references.
Identifiers: LCCN 2018037316 (print) | LCCN 2019006197 (ebook) | ISBN
   9781942094975 (ebook) | ISBN 9781942094968 | ISBN
   9781942094968 (paperback : alk. paper)
Subjects: LCSH: Parents of military casualties--United States. | Parental
   grief--United States.
Classification: LCC UB403 (ebook) | LCC UB403 .S744 2019 (print) | DDC
   355.1/2--dc23
LC record available at https://lccn.loc.gov/2018037316

Photo of Joanne Steen by Sam Hughes Photography. Used with permission.

Cover and interior design by Marisa Jackson.

Table of Contents

Foreword

My wife Carol and I lost our two sons in service to our nation; each died fighting a different kind of battle. Our son Kevin, twenty-one, a senior ROTC cadet at the University of Kentucky and an aspiring Army doctor, died by suicide in June of 2003. Seven months later, our son Jeffrey, twenty-three, an Army Second Lieutenant was killed by an improvised device in Khalidiyah, Iraq in February of 2004. The devastating realization that we had lost one son was the heaviest burden imaginable at the time but the thought that we had lost both of our sons was beyond comprehension. The death of a child no matter the cause is a profound life-changing event for any parent and for us it felt as if our world as we knew it ended twice. For my wife and I, first and foremost, Jeffrey and Kevin were our boys, our sons, and we will mourn their deaths and the permanent loss of their presence in our lives as only parents can. The suddenness of their deaths influenced our early ability to cope with the news. The causes of their deaths impacted what we would contend with for years and years to come. We immediately learned that the stigma surrounding suicide complicated our grief, as much as the death of a soldier in combat did.

We first met Joanne Steen in January of 2008, after I had taken command of Fort Carson and First Army Division West. Joanne was sent to Fort Carson to work with our families of the fallen and educate our chaplains, casualty assistance teams, and unit leaders about military loss and its lasting effect on surviving families and fellow service members.

As a former military instructor, board-certified counselor, and widow of a Navy pilot, Joanne had lived and worked within the military environment. Because she understood the military culture, Joanne provided us with authentic compassion and understanding of our losses, plus reliable guidance and lessons learned on how to survive and cope with the loss of a loved one in service to our nation.

Joanne's presentations to all at Fort Carson filled an unmet need in understanding that a military loss has complicating factors not usually found in civilian losses. She provided all of us with validation that the range of grief reactions we were contending with was not uncommon; in fact, most were quite normal and expected, given the nature of military loss. At that time during the height of the Iraq and Afghanistan Wars when loss and grief were so heavy and ever present at Fort Carson, Joanne was proof that we could not only survive but also move forward with renewed purpose and hope.

In *We Regret to Inform You*, Joanne tackles the subject that parents with a son or daughter currently serving fear the most— the death of their child in military service, regardless of how that death might occur. Well researched and thorough, yet easy to read, this is the book a surviving parent would reach for even at 2:00 a.m. on a sleepless night. Once again Joanne's familiarity with the military culture is evident on every page, as she addresses the pitfalls of military grief in ways only another military survivor could truly understand. Throughout this book, relevant and critical information on grief is reinforced by voices of Gold Star parents, connecting and comforting all who read it.

We Regret to Inform You provides surviving parents with the means to cope and move forward in grief, without fear of leaving the memory of their child behind. Because the loss of a service member touches so many well beyond the immediate family, this book offers relatives, friends, clergy, and other service providers dedicated, informative chapters on what they need to know, what to expect, and what to say to a military survivor in the depths of despair.

My wife Carol and I only wish we had this resource when we were trying to navigate the darkest chapter of our lives. Joanne Steen has poured her heart and soul into the pages of this book and we highly recommend it to every parent who has ever suffered the loss of a child in the military and to anyone whose desire is to bring comfort and support to their broken hearts.

Major General (Retired) Mark Graham, US Army
"Land of the Free . . . Because of the Brave"

The Graham's family story is featured in the book
The Invisible Front: Love and Loss in an Era of Endless War by Yochi Dreazen.

Preface

When a service member dies in the line of duty, the loss has a ripple effect that is felt well beyond the immediate family, extending into the larger circles of relatives, friends, and those who provide professional assistance. We are all moved in some way when we hear the news.

Unknown to many Americans, most military deaths are laden with complications not usually found in civilian losses: a sudden and potentially violent death far from home, limited details and classified information, an unnerving casualty notification process, separation from immediate family by distance or time, soul-searing military traditions to honor the fallen, and an onerous government bureaucracy.

In today's world, there are two widespread beliefs about military loss that are incorrect. The first is that service members only die in war; the second is that military families are prepared for the loss of their loved one. Both are not true.

Since America's earliest days, wars have claimed more than one million military personnel. These war deaths embody the ultimate sacrifice, for service members have lost their lives in the active defense and protection of our rights, freedoms, and homeland. However, war isn't the only time or circumstance in which military personnel die in the line of duty. Service members also lose their lives on other military operations; in protection of our national interests; on peacekeeping missions; from terrorist attacks at home and abroad; in maintaining operational readiness; on training exercises; from equipment failure; because of accidents; by suicide or homicide; or as a result of illness or disease. Approximately three service members die each day with unnoticed regularity.

It is as difficult to explain as it is to understand, but military families are never prepared for that "knock on the door" and the bad news that follows. Today's military families are well aware that military service is an inherently dangerous profession. While families know full well that there's a possibility their service member could be injured or killed, they also know there's a greater probability their loved one will come home safely.

I learned about military loss the hard way. I became a military widow when my husband was killed in the line of duty in peacetime. I assumed there would be resources and support, but both were in short supply. After the 9/11 terrorist attacks and the looming threat of war, I coauthored the book I longed for when my own husband was killed. *Military Widow: A Survival Guide* (Naval Institute Press, 2006), a first-of-its-kind book on military grief, was published at the height of the Iraq War. As a former military instructor, it was natural for me to return to teaching and speaking, this time on the urgently needed topic of casualty response.

After one particular speaking engagement that included Gold Star families, a mother who had lost a son in Iraq approached me and asked when I was going to write a book for Gold Star parents. "Moms and dads need a survival guide too," she said. And she was right.

Many military personnel are married when tragedy strikes, and much attention is given to the new widow and her young family. All too often the needs of the service member's parents go unnoticed. They become outsiders looking in, overwhelmed by the loss of their child, weighed down by both parental and military grief, and chronically misunderstood by those around them.

Gold Star parents learn the hard way that the death of their child in military service changes everything. Family, friends, neighbors, and coworkers, uncertain of what to say or how to act, have a tendency to keep their distance. Even the behavioral health community has limited hands-on experience with, or guidance for, working with military loss.

We Regret to Inform You: A Survival Guide for Gold Star Parents and Those Who Support Them is more than just another book on grief. Until now, no other guide has thoroughly addressed the flag-draped grief that Gold Star parents bear or offered guidance to family, friends, and service providers. This book fills that need.

We Regret to Inform You is a road map for Gold Star parents to survive their life-changing loss, cope with their profound grief, and develop the resilience to move forward.

Family members, friends, and professionals will also find insight and practical advice to support these parents, and the means to increase their confidence and skills in this sensitive area where there is little room for error. A few of the topics covered include:

- Coping with the grief of losing an adult child in an active-duty military status.
- Contending with the perfect storm of military grief.
- Dealing with complicating issues such as unviewable remains, classified information, and deployment-delayed grief.
- Understanding the different ways to grieve.

- Surviving Memorial Day and other important days of meaning.
- Learning why professional service providers need to be informed on military loss.
- Becoming aware of what you need to know, what to expect, and what to say as a relative or friend.

We Regret to Inform You isn't a stuffy, clinical textbook. While it's grounded in the latest research on loss and grief, I use simple, easy-to-understand language throughout the book, as I remember how grief can impair one's ability to take in and retain information. With this in mind, I have kept the chapters short, drawing upon realistic examples and thoughtful explanations to emphasize the important points to remember.

My initial vision for *We Regret to Inform You* was to create a survival guide exclusively for Gold Star parents. But as my research, investigation, and interviews with parents, casualty-assistance personnel, and the behavioral health community progressed, it became clear that for parents to healthfully grieve and move forward, those closest to them must be aware of the lasting impact of a military death and the role they play in the healing of these parents in the long haul. As a result, I have expanded the scope of this book to include families, friends, and professional assistance providers.

Presently, there is limited research on military loss. Those studies that do exist provide a solid starting point, but I also had to rely on the existing research on sudden death and traumatic loss, as more than 80 percent of military deaths are sudden and, frequently, violent in nature.

I conducted an almost obsessive number of interviews with Gold Star parents and had an abundance of conversations with military leaders, casualty-assistance personnel, and medical and behavioral health professionals.

The parents were extraordinary, both in their desire and candor to talk with me about the life-changing loss of their child in military service and in their struggle with the formidable type of grief a military death unleashes. All of the military personnel I met with were equally helpful, some talking about their experiences with military loss for the first time.

This book was difficult to write. Several times during the process, I had to set it aside and recharge my personal batteries. Simply said, what made me persevere was the belief that this book was the right thing to do.

Acknowledgments

It took great courage for the dozens of mothers and fathers to share with me their personal stories of the life, love, and death of their children. To these parents, I remain in awe of your fortitude in the face of unspeakable tragedy, and your desire to help those who will regrettably walk in your shoes one day. My heartfelt thanks and profound gratitude are sent your way. I believe there is a special place in heaven for you and every parent who has been presented with a folded American flag at their child's graveside.

I am especially grateful to the parents and all others who have read sections of this book, providing me with personal insights, advice, and, on occasion, a beneficial redline deletion.

To the spirited Gold Star mothers in the Hampton Roads, Virginia, chapter of the American Gold Star Mothers, I humbly say thank you for all your enthusiastic help along the way. You've shown me what true patriotism looks like and the power of a Gold Star mother's love in action. You are remarkable.

I thank the Department of Defense for helping to make this book for Gold Star parents a reality. I sincerely appreciate the casualty-assistance officers, chaplains, and leaders who spoke openly about their personal experiences with casualty response.

I am grateful to Betsy Beard, surviving mother of Specialist Bradley Beard, US Army, and former editor of the Tragedy Assistance Program for Survivors magazine. I cannot think of a more qualified individual to be my own GPS guide through that perfect storm of military grief that is unleashed by an adult child's death in the military. Your professional expertise, combined with your personal wisdom, was invaluable to me throughout the process.

I offer my heartfelt thanks to Nancy and Mark Stets, Gold Star parents of Staff Sergeant Mark Stets, Jr., US Army. Nancy, you have been my rock in so many ways on this journey, and I am proud to call you a friend. Mark, you have always kept me on my toes with your wry humor.

Special thanks go to Elena Serocki who, once again, worked editing magic on this latest book. Your masterful editing skills and my writing style go together like peanut butter and jelly.

I humbly thank Central Recovery Press for embracing this work and helping to fill the void in grief literature on military loss. I am beholden to my brilliant editor Nancy Schenck, who is a pleasure to work with in every way. Nancy, you have made me sound like a good writer.

And saving the most important thank you for last, I humbly thank my husband Tom. You have provided me with unending patience and support throughout this process. There's truth to the adage that "it's never too late to live happily ever after."

Introduction

To the parents who have lost a son or daughter in the service of our country, I wrote this book for you.

"We regret to inform you." Good news never follows these five words.

The bad news that did follow destroyed life as you knew it, dividing it into two distinct parts: the old days when your child was alive and the hellish reality of a world without your son or daughter.

Most of you had no experience with losing a child and little knowledge of the military. In all likelihood, you were typical, hardworking mothers and fathers, living and working in a civilian community. And you were unaware of the powerful and lasting impact of a military death.

We Regret to Inform You tackles the subject that terrified you—the loss of your child while serving in the military. With an honesty that's found around the kitchen table, this book will help dispel those "Am I going crazy?" thoughts you've probably experienced. It carefully lays out a path through military grief, weaving together real-life examples with understandable explanations.

On these pages, you'll find understanding and validation for many of your feelings, thoughts, and behaviors, as well as the guidance to work through the thorniest issues of military grief:

- Coping with the personal loss of your child and the national loss of a service member.
- Dealing with the perfect storm of military grief that followed your child's death.
- Understanding the different ways you grieve.
- Surviving Memorial Day and other important days of meaning.
- Moving forward, not moving on.
- Developing personal resilience.
- Finding support in communities that do not understand military loss.

This easy-to-read book offers advice and tips to mothers and fathers alike, providing you with not only a head-nodding understanding of your grief, but also guidance on how to develop the resilience to move forward. Using the voices of other Gold Star parents, *We Regret to Inform You* connects you with those who have walked in your shoes.

I hope you will find *We Regret to Inform You* a trustworthy resource for surviving your life-changing loss, coping with its profound grief, and discovering ways to not let grief hold you hostage for the rest of your days.

Thank you for raising good sons and daughters.

Part One

★

Life and Death in the Military

CHAPTER 1

★

America's
Sons and Daughters

"I do solemnly swear that I will support and defend the Constitution of the United States against all enemies, foreign and domestic; that I will bear true faith and allegiance to the same; and that I will obey the orders of the President of the United States and the orders of the officers appointed over me, according to regulations and the Uniform Code of Military Justice. So help me God."

Oath of Enlistment
Armed Forces of the United States

A 2014 Harris poll asked 2,537 adults in the United States what occupations have great prestige. Military service ranked in the top ten, keeping company with firefighters and police officers, nurses and doctors, clergy, and scientists and engineers. It is gratifying to find military service in such esteemed company, for each of these occupations contributes a unique and critical service to the greater good of America and its citizens. All are respected for the dedication and commitment they require.

There is a school of thought that military service is a higher calling, and this poll reinforces that belief. Duty. Honor. Country. These three words are recognized hallmarks of military service and help to define its purpose and identity. When young men and women commit to joining the military, they become part of a purpose greater than themselves. America and its allies rely on our military to protect the peace and, when necessary, defend us from threats and attacks.

THE OATH OF ENLISTMENT AND THE OATH OF OFFICE

By federal law, every man or woman who enlists or reenlists in the US Armed Forces takes an oath of allegiance. Enlisted service members take the oath of enlistment that began this chapter. Officers take the oath of office, which is similar in wording to the oath of enlistment, but also makes reference to the responsibilities of leadership.

The National Guard oaths of enlistment and office are similar to the service branch oaths, but also include allegiance to the state and the state's governor in addition to the federal allegiance to the Constitution and the president.

WHAT THESE OATHS MEAN

If you look closely at the wording of these oaths, you'll see an impressive description of an impressive job. But, as every person who has worn the uniform or loved a service member knows, military service is more than just a job. It's a commitment and sacrifice. It's service to our country by preserving the rights, freedoms, and values found in our Constitution, the foundation of our American way of life. It's protecting our way of life, our national interests, and our homeland, and defending it against all enemies, foreign and domestic. It doesn't matter what uniform your child wore or what specialty, code, or classification he held; each and every job in the military contributes, in some way, to the protection and preservation of America.

America has had an all-volunteer military since the draft ended in 1973. Simply said, no members of the armed forces wear the uniform against their will. Every US service member willingly raised a right hand and, in the presence of a commissioned officer, swore to protect and defend America. Your child chose this path and committed to a block of service time, even when other employment or career options were available. Who knew the son who needed prodding to take out the garbage would one day raise his right hand and voluntarily swear to protect and defend America?

Who knew the son who needed prodding to take out the garbage would one day raise his right hand and voluntarily swear to protect and defend America?

★

PARENT-TO-PARENT

"I told my daughter, if that's what you want to do, then go for it."

A PARENT'S REACTION

America loves a man or woman in uniform, and military parents are on top of that list—they *really* love their sons and daughters in uniform. If you're like most parents, your child's decision to enlist unleashed an assortment of feelings; protecting our country is a dangerous profession, in peacetime and war. How you felt and what you thought about your child's decision likely covered a wide range of feelings—from surprise to pride to terror and everything in between, depending on the day, the circumstance, and which direction the wind was blowing. There's no denying we live in a post-9/11 world. For those whose children have entered the military since then, the reality of homeland terrorist attacks and chronic wars abroad likely factored into your opinion about *your* son or daughter donning the uniform.

PARENT-TO-PARENT

"I was so proud. Then I was worried."

AMERICA'S SONS AND DAUGHTERS

Who are the sons and daughters of America, those who have given their lives in service to our country? They are your children, *your* sons and daughters.

You knew them as only a parent can know a child; you appreciated the strengths and quirks of his personality, you read the expressions on her face, and you recognized the obvious and not-so-obvious potential every child possesses. America knew your children, too. She recognized them, even when she didn't know their names. To her they were:

- The skinny kid who delivered newspapers.
- The high school graduate who was profoundly affected by the 9/11 attacks.
- The young father in need of a steady paycheck in a bad economy.
- The daughter who joined the Navy, just like "dear ol' Dad."
- The hell-raising teen who flunked out of college.
- The young man who always wanted to be a soldier.
- The newest graduate of the Air Force Academy.
- The first-generation immigrant son, looking to make his family proud.
- The son who followed in Dad's Marine Corps footsteps.
- The graduate of the school of "tough love."
- The mom whose National Guard unit was federally activated.
- The middle-aged reservist recalled to active duty.

- The college grad who chose the military over a promising civilian career.
- The father who wanted to show his kids he could make a difference.

These are a few of your children, and they're among the best America has offered to an often-troubled world.

THE PRICE OF FREEDOM

There is an old quote that sums up the depth of a service member's commitment. It's an anonymous quote, which in its humble way makes it applicable to every service member and veteran:

> *A veteran is someone who, at one point in his or her life, wrote a blank check made payable to The United States of America, for an amount of up to and including his or her life. — Source unknown*

It is a powerful message within a sobering statement. And it's true. Every service member knows the day may come when he will find himself in harm's way and perilously close to that fine line between life and death. It's a risk they all choose to live with. In spite of the risks, our military men and women expect to live to a ripe old age. Sometimes, though, life doesn't turn out the way they planned.

... there's a widespread but incorrect belief that service members only die in war.

MILITARY DEATHS

Perhaps because so few Americans have experience with the military, there's a widespread but incorrect belief that service members only die in war.

Since America's earliest days, wars have claimed more than one million military personnel. These war deaths embody the ultimate sacrifice, for service members have lost their lives in the active defense and protection of our rights, freedoms, and homeland. Yet war isn't the only time or circumstance in which military personnel die in the line of duty.

Each year more than 900 soldiers, sailors, airmen, Marines, and coastguardsmen die in service-connected deaths that are not the result of war or terrorism, according to the Department of Defense (DoD). With unnoticed regularity, approximately three service members die

With unnoticed regularity, approximately three service members die each day.

each day. And, since most of these military deaths go unreported in the media, the general public is unaware of the frequency and number of military members who die on active duty.

The year 2001 and the 9/11 terrorist attacks have become the recent baseline for measuring military deaths, even though seventeen sailors were killed when terrorists attacked USS *Cole* (DDG-67) in the harbor of Aden, Yemen, on October 12, 2000. Since that time, more than 23,000 military personnel have died on active duty. While more than 7,000 service members have died as a result of the Iraq and Afghanistan Wars, the majority of military deaths have occurred outside this combat theater of operations, in other locations worldwide. How did your sons and daughters die?

- Killed in action in combat.
- From nonhostile causes in a combat theater.
- In military operations worldwide.
- In support of operational readiness.
- From equipment failures and malfunctions.
- In terrorist attacks.
- On training exercises.
- By suicide or homicide.
- Because of human error.

- In accidents on and off duty.
- From personal misconduct.
- From natural disasters or catastrophes.
- As a result of medical or behavioral health conditions.

SEPTEMBER 11, 2001

On that fated, picture-perfect Tuesday morning, Al Qaeda mass murderers turned hijacked airplanes into weapons, attacking the World Trade Center in New York City and the *September 11* Pentagon in the Washington, DC, area. Another *changed everything.* attack on Washington was prevented when the gutsy passengers and crew aboard hijacked United Airlines Flight 93 fought back, crashing the plane into a rural area outside of Shanksville, Pennsylvania.

By nightfall, chunks of the Pentagon smoldered in fiery ruin, a crater entombed the remains of Flight 93 in a Pennsylvania field, the World Trade Center no longer existed, and Ground Zero emerged from its burning debris. September 11 changed everything. America was now a nation at war.

★

PARENT-TO-PARENT

"Osama bin Laden signed my son's death warrant on 9/11."

A NATION AT WAR

War was something new to your child's generation. The Vietnam War had ended more than forty years ago and the first Gulf War of 1991 lasted forty-four days. Since the United States had not been involved in sustained, ongoing combat for decades, a generation grew up not knowing the real horrors of war.

War was also new to many parents. It became personal when your son or daughter deployed halfway around the world and into a combat zone. In countries mostly unknown to you, nameless bad guys wanted to kill your child, simply because he or she was an American service member and, therefore, the enemy.

THE GLOBAL WAR ON TERROR

In a presidential address to Congress nine days after the September 11 attacks, President George W. Bush stated, "Our war on terror begins with Al Qaeda, but it does not end there. It will not end until every terrorist group of global reach has been found, stopped, and defeated." Shortly after that speech, the phrase Global War on Terror, or GWOT in accepted military language, became the identifiable name of the global efforts to defeat terrorists and prevent future terrorist attacks. The following administration referred to the war on terrorism as Overseas Contingency Operations (OCO), but both terms are infrequently heard now in the national media.

The Global War on Terror was intended to include all terrorist actions. However, it was usually recognized as two wars: the war in Afghanistan and the war in Iraq.

Afghanistan

On October 7, 2001, twenty-six days after the September 11 attacks, an air campaign was launched against Al Qaeda terrorist camps in Afghanistan, beginning what was called Operation Enduring Freedom and the Afghanistan War. Thirteen years later, on December 31, 2014, combat operations officially ended; however, an American military presence remains in Afghanistan as of this writing.

Iraq

On March 20, 2003, about two and a half years after the Afghanistan War began, US and coalition forces commenced military operations in Iraq, initially known as Operation Iraqi Freedom. Eight years later, on December 18, 2011, the US formally declared an end to the Iraq War. As with Afghanistan, American military personnel remain in-country.

DEATHS IN WAR

The Iraq and Afghanistan Wars brought the violence of wartime deaths into civilian homes with graphic images and sobering commentary. Americans were reintroduced to the sacrifices our military personnel make in a time of war, as well as the sacrifices their families make while they wait anxiously on the home front.

The DoD identifies deaths in a war zone as either hostile or nonhostile. But the raw ugliness of war shows through in the descriptions of what constitutes hostile and nonhostile deaths. It's impossible to name every cause of death in war, but here are a few attributed to each classification:

Hostile Deaths
- Improvised explosive devices (IEDs)
- Rocket-propelled grenades (RPGs)
- Firefights
- Sniper attacks
- Ambushes
- Suicide bombs
- Green-on-blue attacks

Nonhostile Deaths
- Friendly fire
- Equipment malfunctions and failure

- Human error
- Accidents
- Ordnance explosions
- Electrocutions and drownings
- Mishaps on land, sea, and air
- Suicides
- Personal misconduct
- Illness and disease

Referring to the deaths of military personnel by category or statistical data sounds impersonal. After all, these service members volunteered to serve our country, even knowing the risks. These men and women were achievers, go-getters, determined and strong. They were your children. And they died too young.

LESSON LEARNED

Protecting America is a dangerous profession—in peacetime and war.

SUMMING IT UP

Your sons and daughters became a part of something greater than themselves when they volunteered for military service. America recognized them as capable soldiers, sailors, airmen, Marines, and Coast Guardsmen. You recognized them as great kids who could make a mother or father proud. And sometimes gray.

CHAPTER 2

Gold Star Parents

I knew.

I knew when I spied the three military men in front of my home.

I knew when I opened the door and saw the look in their eyes: part dread, part sadness, part trepidation.

I knew when the nervous one asked, "Are you Mrs. Smith?"

I knew when the subdued one said, "May we come in?"

I knew as the somber one started to say, "Mrs. Smith, we regret to inform you ..."

I knew. But I didn't believe.

Tanya (Louisiana)

W*e regret to inform you ..."* Good news never follows these five words. The bad news that did follow catapulted you into a world of living hell. It fractured the life you knew, shattering your belief in life's fairness and carving a gaping hole in your heart and psyche. Without exaggeration, this devastating news split your life in two, becoming the permanent divide between the old days when your child was alive and this hellish reality without him or her.

This wasn't supposed to happen. Not now. Not ever. Not to your child. Not to you. But it did, and you're not alone, although it may feel that way. Thousands of parents share your sorrow this day, just as parents did in generations past and, regrettably, as parents will in generations to come.

Thousands of parents share your sorrow this day, just as parents did in generations past and, regrettably, as parents will in generations to come.

Since the dawn of time, men have raised armies for protection and defense. Archeological digs dating back thousands of years have unearthed evidence of weapons and uncovered images of conflict and war. History is filled with accounts of victory and defeat, yet few tell the stories of the families behind the warriors. Nothing has changed.

OPERATIONAL READINESS

The size of the armed forces, often called the end strength, will grow or shrink depending upon the needs of the country. The military usually downsizes after a conflict, maintaining a smaller force in peacetime, and ramps up to engage in war. However, innovations and new technologies are lessening the need for large armies and navies, and recent generations of military forces have gotten smaller, even in times of war.

Out of necessity, the military must maintain a state of operational readiness in order to effectively respond if—or when—a national or global need arises. Keeping the armed forces operationally ready is a dangerous responsibility; military personnel die in support of it every year.

★

PARENT-TO-PARENT

"I don't want my son to be just another nameless military statistic."

THE MILITARY-CIVILIAN GAP

Since the terrorist attacks of 9/11, approximately four million Americans have served in the armed forces—less than 1 percent of the population. Consequently, a separate but parallel world has existed within the United States between the 1 percenters (the military that has functioned at a high operational tempo) and the 99 percenters (the rest of the country that was relatively untouched by terrorism and far removed from conflicts abroad). Most Americans didn't live with the day-to-day anxiety caused by global terrorism and its resulting conflicts—unless your son or daughter was currently serving.

It is safe to say that most of the country is detached from military service.

It is safe to say that most of the country is detached from military service. This growing disconnect has been called the *military-civilian gap*. As a result, the challenges faced by military personnel and their families are often not recognized, much less understood, in the civilian sector. In cities and towns across the country, knowing a service member and the family who loves him or her is the exception rather than the norm.

As the mother or father of a military member who has died on active duty, you contend with the challenge of being an even smaller minority in a population already detached from the military. Who in our country knows who you are?

WHO YOU ARE

Surviving military parents are proud people. You can be found from sea to shining sea and sometimes well beyond. You're not a distant stranger; you're a neighbor, coworker, or family member. You shop at the nearby grocery store, buy gas at the station where your child once worked, and pray at a local church, synagogue, or other place of worship. You live in big cities, small towns, and every area in between.

But who are you? As a surviving parent, you:

- Are relatively young, but old enough to have an adult child.
- Live in the United States or one of its territories, such as Puerto Rico or Guam. You may also live in a country other than the United States. You may not be an American citizen.
- Earn a paycheck in a blue-collar job, a white-collar position, or by other labor. You own your own business. You wear coveralls or a uniform. You don't work outside the home; you may be unemployed or unable to work. Perhaps you're retired.
- Are tall, a little less than tall, or a lot less than tall. You may be of normal weight, be underweight, or carry around a few extra pounds—lots of us do, according to the Centers for Disease Control and Prevention.
- Are white, black or African-American, American Indian or Alaska native, Asian, or native Hawaiian or other Pacific Islander, according to the US Census Bureau. You may be some combination of races or the person who checks "Prefer not to say."
- Are married, widowed, divorced, remarried, single, or in a long-term relationship.
- Are a biological, step-, adoptive, or foster parent.
- Have a family that was intact, scattered, broken, or blended, even before your loss.

Most surviving parents are honest, hardworking moms and dads. Most surviving parents are honest, hardworking moms and dads. In all likelihood, you live and work in a civilian community, so you may not have hands-on experience with, or knowledge of, the military and how it operates. As a surviving parent, you may feel as if you're caught between two vastly different worlds—the military community that your child was a part of and your civilian community that doesn't grasp the powerful consequences of military loss. And in each of these environments, you may feel like an outsider looking in.

Pat, a single parent, described returning to her hometown after her son's funeral as a Wizard of Oz experience. From the notification to the military funeral, "I just hung on and tried to survive the chaos," she said. While Pat was away, something unseen yet fundamental had changed in her hometown, or so she thought. "Even though everything looked the same," she remembered, "I felt I was in a strange and uncomfortable place. Just a few days ago, this was the town where I raised my kids," said *As a Gold Star parent, you bear the burden of living with the sacrifice made by your child.* Pat. Then, almost as an afterthought, she added, "And when I returned, I felt like a visitor in a foreign country. Home didn't feel like home anymore."

The loss of your child in the service of our country left red, white, and blue footprints on your aching heart. As many surviving parents have ruefully said, you are a part of a small club that no mother or father ever wanted to join. You are now the parent of a son or daughter who has died in the service of our country. As a Gold Star parent, you bear the burden of living with the sacrifice made by your child.

★

PARENT-TO-PARENT

"I figured out how to be a dad, but I'll never figure out how to be a Gold Star father."

THE GOLD STAR

All great symbols have a story. And, true to form, so does the gold star. In 1917 during World War I, Army Captain Robert L. Queisser designed a service banner to indicate he had two sons serving on the front lines. His banner, now known as the Blue Star Service Banner, was an 8.5-by-14-inch piece of fabric with a white field framed in red, onto which one or more blue stars were sewn. Each blue star represented a family member currently serving on the front lines. This banner quickly became the unofficial symbol of a family member in military service in wartime.

In a separate event the following year, President Woodrow Wilson approved the use of a gold star on the black mourning armband that was favored by mothers of that era who had lost a son in war. The gold star became the powerful symbol of the ultimate sacrifice made by their sons in wartime. With the approval and use of the gold star on armbands, the tradition blossomed into covering the blue star with a gold one on the service banner, indicating the service member had died in war.

MORE THAN WARTIME DEATHS

During World Wars I and II, these blue star/gold star service banners were widely displayed. In 1947, two years after WWII ended, Congress authorized the creation of a Gold Star Lapel Button (also known as a Gold Star Lapel Pin) for family members whose loved ones died in combat. This pin is a gold star on a field of purple, surrounded by laurel leaves. In 1973, a second lapel pin was approved to recognize the families of service members who died while honorably serving, but not in combat. This pin, a gold star on a gold background surrounded by four oak sprigs, is usually referred to as the Next of Kin Deceased Personnel Lapel Pin and given to families whose loved ones lost their lives on active duty.

AN OFTEN UNRECOGNIZED IDENTITY

The gold star has many meanings in our society. It's commonly recognized as a symbol of achievement or recognition for a job well done. Americans of all ages receive gold stars, from the child whose test score was perfect to the dieter who reached a milestone at a weight loss meeting. Yet, for almost one hundred years, the gold star has also been the symbol of military loss, one that carries with it great pride and shared grief. At the same time, the term *gold star* has evolved into the general identifier of surviving family members who have lost a military member in service to the country. This identity—such as Gold Star mother or Gold Star father—represents all types of military deaths.

... for almost one hundred years, the gold star has also been the symbol of military loss, one that carries with it great pride and shared grief.

Perhaps because the lapel pins were authorized after World War II and were not embraced in the Korean and Vietnam Wars, these pins aren't widely recognized as a symbol of military loss within both civilian and military communities. This has caused a number of awkward moments and hurt feelings for those who proudly wear a military survivor's gold star pin. "I was asked about my gold star pin," explained Janice, "and said I was a Gold Star mother. Then, the person who asked smiled and congratulated me. She had no idea."

While the Gold Star and Next of Kin pins look different, they have much in common. Both pins:

- Have a gold star at the center.
- Represent the life and service of a man or woman who honorably served his or her country.
- Are presented exclusively to surviving family members.
- Convey the pride and shared grief of those who wear either pin.

- Represent how the service member died—a gold star with the purple background signifies a combat death; a gold star with a gold background identifies a death while serving in the military, but not in combat.

LESSON LEARNED

Gold Star parents are regular people trying to cope with an incomprehensible loss.

SUMMING IT UP

One day you were a regular mom or dad, worrying long-distance about your child in the military. Then, without warning, those five little words "We regret to inform you . . ." shattered life as you knew it.

Now you're a Gold Star parent who has lost your child to death, and you're trying to survive and cope within this unending nightmare.

Part Two

★

A
Life-Changing
Loss

★

CHAPTER 3

Loss of Your Son or Daughter

I learned that my son Alonso had been killed while I was in the parking lot of a home improvement store. I had just pulled into a parking space when one of his high school buddies texted me how sorry he was to hear the news. I didn't know what he was talking about, so I called my wife. Apparently, it was all over social media about a serious mishap in Al's squadron. Those first posts weren't good. Bad news travels fast, I guess.

Around suppertime, the Air Force came to our door. At first, I wanted to believe they were coming to tell us that Al was okay, but that wasn't the case. He was one of nine squadron members who were killed. The casualty team didn't have too much to tell us about what had happened, though. That part of the bad news didn't travel fast.

Later that night, I sat alone in the dark, feeling utterly helpless. The Air Force just notified us that our son was dead. I told them I wanted to go to where Alonso was killed and help out. But they said they had skilled personnel for just this purpose and everything was under control. They assured my wife and me that our son's remains would be coming home soon.

I told them they didn't understand—a boy always needs his dad when times are bad.

Manny (California)

Grief experts agree: there is no greater loss than the death of a child, regardless of whether the child is an infant, a teenager, or an adult in uniform. The extraordinary bonds between a parent and a child create a relationship unlike any other. Powerful physical and emotional bonds, strong social and behavioral bonds, and deep spiritual and intuitive bonds all fuse a parent to a child and, likewise, a child to a parent. There aren't enough words in the English language—or any language, for that matter—that can fully convey the scope of the parent-child bond or the depth of a parent's anguish over losing a child. For surviving parents, the agony of losing a son or daughter is unspeakably heartbreaking, often described as a fate worse than death. But you already know this from firsthand experience.

AN UNNATURAL LOSS

The death of your son or daughter violated the order of nature. Your child was not supposed to die before you. This isn't how you counted on life to work out. It was unnatural for your child to die first, and

Your child was not supposed to die before you. This isn't how you counted on life to work out.

that makes the death harder to comprehend and eventually adjust to. You'll likely spend the rest of your life learning to live with the loss of your son or daughter. Most surviving parents do.

You were connected to your child in countless ways, many of which were obvious, while others you may not have realized yet. Each way you were connected represents a piece of your loss, much like the pieces of a jigsaw puzzle. In its box, the puzzle is in hundreds of little pieces, each just a fraction of the big picture. As these puzzle pieces are matched together, a bigger picture begins to emerge. It takes time, perseverance, and patience to figure out how all the pieces fit into the big picture. And so it is with the hundreds of losses that came from the death of your child.

PRIMARY LOSSES

It is impossible to name all the losses that originated from your child's death. You felt some of the primary losses immediately; others you became aware of in the weeks, months, and years afterward. The primary losses you most likely faced because of your son or daughter's death include:

- Loss of part of your past, present, and future.
- Loss of a physical part of yourself.
- Loss of a physical part of your family.
- Loss of emotional interaction with your child.
- Loss of your role and identity as a parent.

Loss of a Part of Your Past, Present, and Future

As a parent, you lost a part of your past, present, and future when your child died. You lost a little boy or girl, once so innocent and trusting, who was totally dependent on you. You were the "fixer" to this little one, for you had the power to make everything right in his world. You lost a teenager, who you swore on several occasions was really an alien sent from a faraway planet. This was the teenager who tested your patience and sometimes your sanity, and secretly reminded you of yourself at that age—a detail you had never planned to reveal. You lost a good young woman, one whom you watched mature into an increasingly responsible adult after the aliens departed for parts unknown. You had high hopes for your child and were eager to see what she would make of the future. You lost the chance to have an adult relationship with your son and be a part of the normal, continuing cycle of life within your family. And you lost the adult daughter of your later years, the one you would have turned to when the process of aging got too hard to handle.

★

PARENT-TO-PARENT

"I can't fix this."

Loss of a Physical Part of Yourself

For most biological parents, there was never a time when you weren't a part of your son or daughter's life. Your child was a part of you, your own flesh and blood. Your son was a unique creation of you and your spouse or partner. He possessed many of your traits and characteristics and, to a lesser extent, traits and characteristics from both sets of grandparents. To figure out where your son got his laughing brown eyes, you had only to look at his mother—or look in the mirror. Wonder where your daughter got her curly red hair? Check out pictures of Grandma. With your child's death, a physical part of you and your spouse died, as did parts of your own parents and grandparents that had been passed down through your family tree.

> *It didn't matter whether your child was a married adult with a family of his own, or still living under your roof; your child held an important place among those you call family.*

Loss of a Physical Part of Your Family

In addition to losing a part of yourself, you lost the physical presence of your son or daughter and all that your child brought into your life. It didn't matter whether your child was a married adult with a family of his own, or still living under your roof; your child held an important place among those you call family.

Families come in all shapes and sizes, from the single parent with an only child to the blended families of the "yours, mine, and ours" variety. What's most important is that your child was a part of *your* family.

Loss of Emotional Interaction with Your Child

As a parent, you loved your child deeply and unconditionally. It's been said there is no greater love than the love of a parent for a child. Your love for your child has no expiration date. It runs deep; it runs strong; and it lasts forever.

Your emotional connection with your child began long before birth. Your child made his presence known to you from the earliest days of pregnancy. You started to become a parent when you provided for and protected your unborn little one. If you're the biological mother, you most likely sought medical care, changed your diet, modified your behavior, created a safe and comfortable home, carried on one-sided conversations with your unborn child, and responded to kicks, hiccups, and a few unmentionable noises known only to you.

Your love for your child has no expiration date. It runs deep; it runs strong; and it lasts forever.

As your son or daughter grew up, you were emotionally connected to your child's dreams, goals, achievements, and failures. When your son was happy, you were happy; when your daughter was hurting, you hurt, too. Like many moms and dads, you would sometimes sense that something was amiss with your child, even without words being spoken.

Perhaps you were a parent who had a strained or broken relationship with your son or daughter. Regardless of the situation, you still had an emotional connection to your child. When your son or daughter died, you lost not only your child but also the chance to make the relationship right again.

Loss of Your Role and Identity as a Parent

You didn't stop being a parent when your child died. Once a parent, always a parent. While you may have been finished with the job of raising your son into adulthood, a mother or father is never done with parenting. It's guaranteed lifetime employment. The scope

You didn't stop being a parent when your child died.

of your parental radar may have broadened considerably when your child became an adult, but it also had a long-lasting battery life.

With the loss of a child, moms and dads wrestle with their identity as parents. "I still get stopped in my tracks when people ask me how many children I have," said Vanessa, "and when certain people ask it, that question remains too hard to answer."

For surviving parents, there is no single identity, no one term, that identifies you as a parent who has lost a child in the same way the words *widow* or *widower* identify a surviving spouse.

★

PARENT-TO-PARENT

"I wasn't done raising my baby."

SECONDARY LOSSES

Secondary losses are real losses stemming directly from the death of your child. Initially, you may not have been aware of the concept of secondary losses, the number of these losses that faced you, or the power found in them. But as the sobering reality of your devastating loss began to sink in, you were confronted with additional, unanticipated losses brought about by the death of your child. As time unfolds, it will seem like many more things have been taken away from you.

In the spring 2013 volume of *TAPS Magazine,* Jill Harrington-LaMorie, DSW, LCSW, described secondary losses in terms of tossing a pebble into a still pond. As the pebble strikes the pond's surface and sinks to the bottom, it disturbs the water around it, causing an expanding ripple effect of motion in the surrounding water. "Death has that ripple effect as well," Harrington-LaMorie explained, "setting off a disturbance that moves across time and space."

It is normal to have feelings of grief over your secondary losses. In fact, it's healthy to do so. Your secondary losses are real. They cause pain in the present and also in the future.

It is normal to have feelings of grief over your secondary losses. In fact, it's healthy to do so. Your secondary losses are real.

Because of the individuality of your son or daughter and the relationship you had with your child, it's impossible to list every secondary loss you have already experienced—or may come across in the years to come. But, like other surviving military parents, you may have felt the loss of:

- Being called Mom or Dad again.
- Your "old" spouse who, like yourself, was changed by the death of your child.
- Contact, or reduced contact, with your grandchildren.
- The roles your son held in your life and you in his.
- Contact with your daughter's friends in her military unit.
- Your child's beloved pet when it crossed over the Rainbow Bridge.
- Shared interests or hobbies with your son or daughter.
- Your family surname passed down to another generation.
- Becoming a grandmother or grandfather.
- Family and friends who faded away.
- Your child's sexual orientation, when an unexpected one came to light afterward.
- Your own identity.

- Faith in the government and/or the military for putting your child in harm's way.
- Trust in a predictable world.
- Feeling protected from harm.
- Deep-rooted spiritual beliefs.
- Peace of mind.
- Control.

It is important to understand that a number of your secondary losses are tangible, such as the loss of your son's favorite dog, which may have been a powerful connection to him. Other secondary losses are subtler, or intangible, such as the realization that life isn't fair or just.

It is also important to recognize that each of these circumstances is a loss and generates authentic grief feelings. Don't try to minimize these losses, ignore them, or rationalize them away.

LESSON LEARNED

Your child's death is the beginning of countless losses for you.

SUMMING IT UP

The crushing loss of your son or daughter is a fate worse than death. It is an unnatural loss, a violation of the order of nature, regardless of your child's age or marital status.

Your child's death was only the beginning of the losses you will experience, as you become aware of secondary losses in the weeks, months, and years afterward. And each of these losses brings another sobering reminder that your son or daughter is dead.

★

CHAPTER 4

How Your Child Died Shapes Your Grief

We hold these truths to be self-evident, that all men are created equal, that they are endowed by their Creator with certain unalienable Rights, that among these are Life, Liberty and the pursuit of Happiness.

The Declaration of Independence
Philadelphia, Pennsylvania
July 4, 1776

America's Declaration of Independence boldly proclaims that all men are created equal. Ironically, the deaths of all men are not equal in predictability, trauma, or impact.

How your child died, its level of expectedness, and the surrounding circumstances had a major effect on not only your initial reaction to the news, but also how you cope with it in the years to come. You probably haven't given much thought to how people die. It's a subject that doesn't come up often in conversation. It's important to learn about it now, as it can help you to better understand your past reactions, as well as your present and future ones.

Death is divided into two general categories: anticipated death and sudden death. Each presents hurdles for survivors.

YOUR CHILD DIED AN ANTICIPATED DEATH

An anticipated death is most often associated with illness, disease, or old age. It occurs when there is no hope of recovery, and the end of life is on the horizon. Illnesses and diseases accounted for 18 percent of all active-duty deaths, according to the Department of Defense.

If your active-duty son was diagnosed with a life-threatening illness, predictably it was a shock to you. As a service member, he was in excellent physical shape, and you probably felt his physical conditioning and youthful resilience were enough of a catalyst to fight this illness and eventually recover. Death was an unthinkable outcome. After all, your son was young and strong. At some point, even as you hoped and prayed for a cure, it began to dawn on you that he may not recover. Whether you realized it or not, you likely started to prepare for the possibility of his death.

An anticipated death is most often associated with illness, disease, or old age. It occurs when there is no hope of recovery, and the end of life is on the horizon.

A heartbreaking frustration with an anticipated death is knowing your child will die soon, watching him slip away, and being powerless to stop it. Knowing your son was living out his last days did not—in any way, shape, or form—make his death easier to accept or lessen your pain.

If your son's death was anticipated, you hopefully had the chance to be physically present at his bedside and saw firsthand that his condition was grave. It's tough to see your son suffer; it's even tougher for a parent to be unable to save him. Possibly, you had the chance to be the caregiving mom or dad again, reassure your son that you loved him, and learn of any last wishes he wanted to have carried out. But did you say goodbye? Probably not. As the late Darcie Sims, PhD, grief counselor, bereaved mother, and friend to families of the fallen, often said, "You say I love you, but you never say goodbye."

★

YOUR CHILD DIED A SUDDEN DEATH

A sudden death is usually attributed to a natural cause or a human cause. In most cases, it occurs without forewarning to the service member and the survivors. Some naturally caused sudden deaths originate from within, such as respiratory failure or cardiac arrest; others come from Mother Nature, such as an earthquake or other natural phenomena. In all of these cases, there was no ill will or hostility that contributed to the service member's death.

Human-caused sudden deaths are due to the direct or indirect actions of another person or a group of people. These actions include war, terrorism, military operations, accidents, negligence, misconduct, suicide, and homicide. More than 80 percent of military deaths are sudden ones.

If your child died suddenly, you had no time to emotionally prepare for it. The shock of your child's death undoubtedly left you feeling stunned and overwhelmed and, possibly, helpless and powerless.

A sudden death is usually attributed to a natural cause or a human cause. In most cases, it occurs without forewarning to the service member and the survivors.

Shock possesses a sneaky and incapacitating power, and odds are it compromised your ability to take in the news and your emotional means to cope with it. In all likelihood, denial became your newest friend. That's not necessarily a bad thing at that place and time because denial allowed you to absorb, in small, tolerable doses, the shock of the news about your daughter.

The sudden death of your daughter robbed you of the chance to be with her in the last few moments of life. You were cheated out of holding or hugging her, telling your daughter how much you loved her, giving or seeking forgiveness, and just being a parent to your daughter one last time.

PARENT-TO-PARENT

"I was there when she was born and I should've been there when she died."

TRAUMATIC DEATH

There is a subset of sudden death called traumatic death, in which the death is violent in nature and results in massive damage to, or destruction of, the body. A leading expert on traumatic loss, Therese Rando, PhD, explained the concept of traumatic death in her book *How to Go on Living when Someone You Love Dies,* Rando identified some general conditions that define a death as traumatic:

- Sudden and unexpected.
- Random or preventable.
- Violent death, with damage to the body.
- One of several deaths occurring together.
- Survivor's safety was personally threatened.
- Survivor had a personal encounter with the violent death.[1]

However, through the eyes of a parent, the death of a son or daughter is traumatic, regardless of its circumstances.

PARENT-TO-PARENT

"Don't tell me I can't see my son's body, and stop referring to it as 'remains'!"

---

[1] Therese A. Rando, *How to Go on Living when Someone You Love Dies* (New York: Bantam, 1991).

SUDDEN TRAUMATIC DEATH IN THE MILITARY

Many sudden deaths in the military are violent ones. Combat, terrorist attacks, and numerous accidents, homicides, and suicides are violent in nature, resulting in catastrophic damage, dismemberment, or destruction of the service member's body.

With the arrival of a military casualty team and the news they brought with them, your first response was probably similar to that of other military parents, which was one of disbelief. "I told the casualty team it wasn't possible that my son is dead," recounted Pam, "and then I rattled off three perfectly good reasons why this news couldn't be true."

Because of the mission of the armed forces, a military death has its own baggage, some of which isn't found in a civilian sudden death. These complications contributed to your inability to believe—much less accept—the devastating news that your child is dead, especially in the emotionally numb days after your notification. Complications of a military death include:

- **An official, but secondhand, account.** Your casualty team was acting in an official capacity for your son's service branch, and the news it delivered was provided by the service branch casualty office. In almost all instances, neither your casualty team nor the casualty office personnel were on-site when your son died. Thus, you didn't have the testimony of a firsthand account of what took place before, during, and after his death.

- **No tangible proof.** You had no immediate physical proof that this terrible news was true; there was nothing you could see, touch, or smell that belonged to your son—nothing that indicated great harm had come to him.

- **Distant death site.** When your son died, most likely he was stationed in another part of the country or deployed outside the United States. This eliminated any chance to immediately get to the physical scene of his death.

- **Time delay.** If your son died violently or there were multiple deaths or his death occurred in a remote or dangerous spot, it may have taken several days to retrieve his remains before releasing them for burial or interment.

The utter shock of your child's sudden death, combined with these factors that are usually a part of military loss, may have so overwhelmed you that your basic ability to function in your daily life was hampered for a time. Some moms and dads become so distraught that they can't carry out common tasks or make necessary decisions.

A number of parents described operating on autopilot, functioning like a robot without emotions. Each circumstance is a normal reaction to a child's death. Each also contributes to the escalating anxiety and stress in and around you at a time when emotions are already stretched to the breaking point.

★

PARENT-TO-PARENT

"My son did not 'pass away.' He was killed—there's a big difference!"

UNKNOWN AND UNKNOWABLE DETAILS

Initial details of most sudden deaths are sparse, in both the military and civilian sectors. But, honestly, there are *never* too many details for surviving parents.

You may have felt you were left without a clear understanding of the events that led up to your child's death or the details of it. A number of surviving parents feel this way. In fact, it's common for parents to become obsessed with finding out every detail that led up to and included the death, particularly a sudden, traumatic one.

As the parent of a child who has died from any cause, you've probably reconstructed and replayed in your mind the final moments of your child's death more times than you can count. You tried to piece together his last actions with the information you had at hand; you stumbled over the gaps in that story and hunted for the information to fill them in. The how and why of it consumed you.

Nonsurvivors probably thought this was morbid and urged you to "let it go." Grief professionals would say that early in your grief, this obsession is therapeutic and important to your healing. At some point, as you replayed all those details yet again, your psyche came to expect the end of the story—your child died—and this obsession started to lose its control over you.

It's a tragic reality, but you may never learn every detail of what happened when your child died.

What happens when you never learn all of the details of your child's death? This occurs more often than you may realize in both civilian and military deaths. It's a tragic reality, but you may never learn every detail of what happened when your child died. It's important to grasp this sobering fact. The challenge it creates for you is to accept the death—given the details and information you have—and work to *make your peace* with it.

On a personal note, as a Gold Star widow, I know how that need for answers can consume days and nights, as I struggled with my need for answers for a very long time. Eventually, I came to realize that I'd never know exactly how my late husband and his six-man crew were killed, except that their helicopter exploded in midair. With that realization, I worked hard to make my peace with the set of circumstances and the explanation that I had available. Is it 100 percent accurate? Who knows? But for the sake of my sanity, I chose to be okay with it.

LESSON LEARNED

There is no good way for your child to die,
but some ways are worse than others.

SUMMING IT UP

Your child's death is a painful, personal loss regardless of whether it was anticipated or sudden. But the suddenness of it, the cause, and its circumstances influenced how you reacted initially, what you're coping with now, and what you'll likely contend with in the future.

CHAPTER 5

★

Ten Factors That Complicate Your Military Loss

I was relieved when my son, Jesse, told my ex-husband and me that his new orders didn't send him back to the Middle East. He wasn't happy about it, but we were. After two deployments there, Jesse was finally stationed in a place where people weren't regularly trying to kill him or his buddies. I finally relaxed a bit, about as much as a mom with a kid in today's military can relax.

I heard about the bombing of the military installation where Jesse was stationed on the morning news. I told myself the chances were slim that he was involved, but a parent always worries. Time dragged at work, but I figured the more hours that passed by, the greater the chances my son was okay. I guess I figured wrong.

Just before the end of my shift, my boss told me I needed to get home ASAP. By the time I got there, my daughter was waiting on the front porch. I never noticed the white sedan parked down the street.

Here I am, now three years out, and I still can't comprehend that my baby was killed by an explosion so fierce that only fragments of his body were recovered. I never got to see my son again.

Therese (New York)

The death of a son or daughter is always an overwhelming loss to a parent. Often thwarted by emotional devastation and unspeakable grief, any parent—military or civilian—is challenged by this loss. But when the death occurs because of military service, this grief-laden challenge is often weighed down with additional factors. To help you understand your multifaceted loss better, I'll discuss ten factors that complicate a military death. These factors are grouped into three key areas:

- Life and death of the service member.
- Current life circumstances of the survivors.
- America and military service.

★ ★ ★ ★ ★ ★ **Life and Death of the Service Member** ★ ★ ★ ★ ★ ★

1. Service member was young.	*3. Often died a sudden, traumatic death.*
2. He or she led a purposeful life.	*4. Sometimes died on deployment.*

LIFE AND DEATH OF THE SERVICE MEMBER

To gain a better personal understanding of why a military death is complicated, let's start by looking at a few characteristics of the service member. Then we must take into account how the death occurred and its location.

Here's why these first four factors strongly influence your reactions to the death of your military son or daughter.

1. **The service member was young.** There's an old saying that military service is a young man's—and now a young woman's—game. A look at the age of our military confirms this as true:

   - Thirty years old or younger: 66 percent of the total active-duty force.
   - Twenty-five years old or younger: 50 percent of the enlisted active-duty force.

Our service members *are* young. They're also in good physical shape, well trained, and well equipped. Top off their age, fitness, equipment, and training with a healthy dose of enthusiasm, and our service members think they're invincible. That's a good thing, because it's normal and expected for young men and women to think this way, according to developmental psychologists.

As the parent of a service member, you saw your child as strong and skilled, too. When your young, capable son died, you undoubtedly struggled with the disconnect between youthful invincibility and death. In those early days of shock and disbelief, you probably asked yourself and anyone else within earshot, "How could my young, healthy, and strong son be dead?"

★

PARENT-TO-PARENT

"My baby was only nineteen."

2. **The service member led a purposeful life.** Military service has an important purpose in our troubled world. Our service members understand the importance of this purpose and, to the best of their ability, each willingly contributes to it. Ask a service member who he works for and most likely he'll tell you, "I serve my country." Ask a service member why she puts on the uniform and there's a good chance she'll say, "It's the right thing to do." Ask any service member why he or she will go into harm's way and you'll probably hear, "It's my job."

When your child died, it was a personal loss to you and your family and a public loss to society.

When your child died, it was a personal loss to you and your family *and* a public loss to society. At a young age, your child had already made a meaningful contribution to the greater good. Our society was robbed of this valued member who had the potential to contribute much more.

3. The service member may have died a sudden, traumatic death.

Most military deaths are sudden ones. If your son died a sudden and violent death, you had to contend with the unexpectedness of the death, the preventability or

You may have feared for your child's safety, but you anticipated he would live and eventually make his way home.

deliberateness of it, and the known or unknown damage inflicted on his body, especially if it wasn't viewable or recoverable. These factors had a great influence on how you reacted initially, and what you struggle with now and will struggle with in the future.

You didn't send your son out the door and potentially into harm's way expecting him to die. While you may have feared for his safety—especially if he had a high-risk occupation or went off to war—you anticipated he would live and eventually make his way home.

★

PARENT-TO-PARENT

"My son's remains came home to me four separate times."

4. The service member possibly died on deployment or in another operation.

Deployments and military operations are a necessary part of the military's job. They occur for peacekeeping purposes, armed combat, deterrence, and humanitarian needs; to show the flag; and to pre-position military assets in the world's hot spots.

If your daughter died on deployment or in some other military operation, you likely dealt with a distant scene of death, limited details and information, and the transportation of her body back to the States. There was little you could do but sit and wait. Because the recovery and identification of remains are a part of the military's casualty process, you had no influence over this process, even though this was your daughter.

★

PARENT-TO-PARENT
"She was twenty-two days away from the end of her deployment."

★ ★ ★ ★ ★ **Current Life Circumstances of the Survivors** ★ ★ ★ ★ ★

5. *Young families left behind.*   7. *Subject to deployment-delayed grief.*
6. *Isolated by geography.*

CURRENT LIFE CIRCUMSTANCES OF THE SURVIVORS

The life circumstances of surviving family members are as much contributing factors to complicating military loss as are the life and death of the service member. Your age, your location, and, possibly, your child's location at the time of death are inextricably linked to your grief.

5. **Young families left behind.** Most of the military is under thirty, as you've read on the previous pages. That's young, especially in the eyes of a parent. Fallen service members often leave behind younger, middle-aged mothers and fathers, living grandparents, and, often, young spouses, some of whom are pregnant or have young children. With the US life expectancy close to eighty years old, it's possible your child's

death was the first one within your immediate family.

As a surviving parent dealing with the death of your adult child, you may find yourself sandwiched between raising younger dependent children and looking after aging parents. It's also possible you have assumed legal guardianship for your late son or daughter's children. All of these obligations serve to compound your grief.

★

PARENT-TO-PARENT

"No parent should have to endure a child's funeral."

6. **Isolated by geography.** The odds are high that you don't live near your son's last duty station. Consequently, when tragedy struck, you were without the immediate support of those who understood the military culture and its way of doing things, or of those personnel who served with your son. With so few serving in today's armed forces, there's a very good chance your circle of family and friends are not familiar with, or equipped to handle, the multiple sides of your military loss. As a result, you are isolated not only from the military by geography, but also within your primary support system of family and friends. They don't know how to help you with this complex and public loss.

... when tragedy struck, you were without the immediate support of those who understood the military culture and its way of doing things ...

7. **Deployment-delayed grief.** When a service member was *supposed* to be on deployment, surviving family members find it harder to believe that the service member has died, especially before deployment ended, a closed-casket funeral was necessary, or no body was recovered.

If your son died on deployment, you may have held onto a glimmer of hope that the military had made a mistake and he would come home with the rest of the returning forces when the deployment ended. Some people call this denial; others recognize it as a reality of military loss.

★

PARENT-TO-PARENT

"For a time, I honestly believed my son was on a secret mission."

When your son's unit returned home without him, it extinguished the last flicker of hope you carried within you that—somehow—he was still alive. The unit's homecoming without him was a harsh dose of reality. Whether or not you attended it, it's common for this homecoming to have generated some exceptionally strong emotions and feelings of grief for you. They may have been as strong as the ones you felt in the early days after you were notified.

If your son died on deployment, you may have held onto a glimmer of hope that the military had made a mistake and he would come home with the rest of the returning forces when the deployment ended.

★ ★ ★ ★ ★ ★ ★ ★ **America and Military Service** ★ ★ ★ ★ ★ ★ ★ ★

8. National loss and a personal loss.
9. National reminders of military death.
10. Recognition and identity.

AMERICA AND MILITARY SERVICE

Many significant historical events in the history of America have military roots, from the American Revolution of 1776 to the Civil War of 1861 to the September 2001 terrorist attacks. These events, and many more like them, have shaped the country's perception of military service.

Following are the last of the ten factors that complicate military loss:

8. **A national loss and a personal loss.** While the nation was burying a valued service member, you were burying your child. You knew him not by rank and last name, but by the name or nickname you gave to him. In your eyes, your son was your child first and then a military member. Because your son was a valued service member, he received military funeral honors rendered to only a select group of Americans.

A military funeral is America's ceremonial way of paying respect.

A military funeral is America's ceremonial way of paying respect. It is a time-honored tribute, profound and powerful, from a grateful nation to a service member or veteran who has honorably served in times of war or peace.

Alan Wolfelt, PhD, noted author and grief counselor, has often said that ritual gives meaning to ceremony. In this light, a military funeral is in a class by itself. It renders for all to witness the honor and respect fittingly due a service member or veteran.

A military funeral is a public event, and its rituals are etched onto military and civilian hearts alike: the military honor guard, the flag-draped casket, the crisp resonance of the rifle salute, the haunting notes of "Taps," and the precision of folding the casket flag. Once folded into a triangle of white stars on a sea of blue, the flag is presented to the family with the timeless message, "On behalf of the president of the United States, the [United States Army, United States Navy, United States Marine Corps, United States Air Force, or

United States Coast Guard], and a grateful nation, please accept this flag as a symbol of our appreciation for your loved one's honorable and faithful service."

9. **National reminders of military deaths.** America has two federal holidays to honor its service members. Memorial Day honors the fallen in May and Veterans Day remembers all veterans, living and dead, on November 11. These are days when America publicly acknowledges the sacrifices of the Armed Forces with tributes, parades, and services of remembrance and gratitude. Memorial Day comes once a year, but as a surviving mom or dad, you know all too well that every day is a memorial day.

> *Memorial Day comes once a year, but as a surviving mom or dad, you know all too well that every day is a memorial day.*

★

PARENT-TO-PARENT

"It's not my birthday—don't wish me a 'Happy' Memorial Day."

As a Gold Star parent, you may take offense at the commercialization of Memorial Day. All too often, it's seen as nothing more than a three-day weekend and the unofficial start of summer. The true purpose of Memorial Day is often usurped by cookouts and sales events.

Becoming the parent of a fallen service member has undoubtedly changed how you look at America. Symbols of our country, embedded in the collective American subconscious, may now magnify your loss in ways never imagined by the nonsurvivor community. That American flag fluttering in the breeze is a pride-filled, yet sometimes anguished, personal reminder of your son or daughter. How about the "Star-Spangled Banner" that puts patriotism to music and is sung at countless ceremonies and events? It can ignite an emotional reaction in you when you least expect it,

Symbols of our country, embedded in the collective American subconscious, may now magnify your loss...

just as easily as a thirty-second news clip about a military homecoming can. These responses, and many others like them, are common among Gold Star parents. Who knew how often military scenes showed up in the news media or entertainment industry?

A profound and sometimes traumatic reminder of your loss is hearing the mournful melody of "Taps." Anytime. Anywhere. Only another survivor can truly understand how deeply personal those somber notes become after you've experienced a bugler blowing "Taps" for your own loved one.

There are several verses to "Taps," yet it is rarely, if ever, sung at a funeral or memorial. "I don't need to hear the words to 'Taps,'" said Lou. "That melody is powerful enough."

10. **A level of recognition and identity.** As the surviving parent of a service member who has died since 9/11, you may have experienced public support and, possibly, media attention. If your son or daughter was killed in action or died in a military operation, you may have become the public identity of military loss in your community.

This combination of a public identity as a Gold Star parent and the media attention of a high-profile death may have become a double-edged sword for you. On one hand, the publicity gives you the opportunity to tell the world about your child. It helps keep the memory of him alive. On the other hand, this type of attention can keep you in an acute grief mode, stuck in the grief that the media expects to see in a Gold Star parent. It's easy to get caught up in it. Unknowingly, you may have become stuck in your grief, and in not making progress through its toughest parts into a more livable level of it.

If your child didn't die in hostile warfare but died by another means while on active duty, you may feel that his death was perceived as less relevant or important. To some degree, the death of your son may not have been fully recognized within your community of family and friends—or even other military survivors. Your identity as a Gold Star parent may not have been properly acknowledged or supported. As a result, your son's death—as well as your grief—may be disenfranchised.

Combat deaths embody the ultimate sacrifice, for service members have lost their lives in the active defense and protection of our rights, freedoms, and homeland.

Combat deaths embody the ultimate sacrifice, for service members have lost their lives in the active defense and protection of our rights, freedoms, and homeland. It's important to keep in mind that service members also die in the line of duty in times of peace. Military service is a purposeful but dangerous profession, and as you read in Chapter One, roughly three service members die each day with unnoticed regularity.

Every military death is a loss to our nation. Our country honors and appreciates all of its service members who have honorably served or have died because of that service. A testament of that appreciation is the folded flag presented to surviving family members from a grateful nation.

LESSON LEARNED

*The grief generated from a military death is complex,
complicated, and just plain messy.*

SUMMING IT UP

A military death is often fraught with uncommon circumstances and
assorted hurdles for a surviving parent, as you've read in this chapter
and experienced in your own grief. Each of these ten factors on its
own can be complicating; undoubtedly, most, if not all, are woven
into your personal grief.

As a Gold Star mother or father, you grieve a dual loss: the death
of your child and the death of a valued service member. This dual
loss is one few understand.

Part Three

★

Survival

CHAPTER 6

★

A Parent's Grief

I figured at this point in my life there was nothing that could rattle me. I'd been on this planet long enough to have seen and done it all. That's what I thought. Then came the news about my son, Ricky. I gotta admit, going to that military base in Dover to see Ricky's casket come home to America just about killed me. But it was back here in Texas—I think it was in the middle of his funeral—when I figured out that I'd probably die soon, too. And I was okay with that.

A couple of days later, I was fiddling around in the garage when the terrible thought struck me that I might not die right now. And I wondered, how was I going to live in this world without my boy?

Don (Texas)

We live in a society that avoids death and grief.

This wasn't always the case in the United States. At the turn of the twentieth century, people were more exposed to death as a natural part of life. The nuclear family often shared living spaces with its extended family, and multiple generations lived under one roof. Families rarely dispersed or relocated. In most families of that era, a baby or two was born each year and an elderly member or two died, just like clockwork. Death wasn't reserved only for the elderly, though. A host of diseases robbed the young and middle-aged of life, as well as accidents and the ravages of World Wars I and II. Funerals were community events that included the immediate and extended family, as well as the neighbors and faith community, for the bonds created in these tight-knit communities were as close as family. Children and adults learned about grief on a day-to-day basis by living with the bereaved as a family member or neighbor. While they may have been uncomfortable with death, they certainly had been exposed to it—and also to the grief that followed.

In today's twenty-first century, death and grief are more removed from everyday life. A smaller number of people die in their homes. Those tight-knit communities of earlier times are few and far between. Family members are more transient, often scattered across the United States and abroad, sometimes by choice and other times by necessity, such as a duty station assignment. Because of this transience, extended family members, neighbors, and acquaintances are less likely to feel the weight of a death and less inclined to offer the longer-term support needed by bereaved families. Grieving family members often become isolated in their loss. Their needs, as well as their actions, are poorly understood. As society changed in the past hundred years, there was less exposure to death in general, less experience with it personally, and fewer public and private role models of grief and mourning behaviors.

LEARNING ABOUT GRIEF

It's important for you to learn about grief. Why, you may ask? Isn't living with grief all the real-life knowledge one needs? Not quite.

Although you may have been familiar with grief from other losses in your life, you may not have been aware of how deeply parental grief affects your health, your relationships, and your well-being. Additionally, the death of your military son or daughter didn't come with an instruction manual on grief, particularly the multidimensional grief that usually goes hand in hand with a military death.

Thanatologists, the professionals who study death and our responses to it, define grief in many ways. Grief has been described as an array of emotions, thoughts, and reactions to loss. It also has been characterized as a process or journey through the realization of a loss and the adjustment to it. Both are correct. However, even though death is a worldwide occurrence, there can be no single description for grief, no one-size-fits-all definition that works for everyone.

... the death of your military son or daughter didn't come with an instruction manual on grief, particularly the multidimensional grief that usually goes hand in hand with a military death.

Simply said, grief is hard to describe. And trying to describe it depends on whether you're an outsider looking in or an insider trying to escape. You probably didn't think about how it was described when your child died. Like relatives who have long overstayed a visit, you just wanted grief to go away and leave your old life alone—exactly as it was. It doesn't work that way.

GRIEF

In its simplest form, grief is a natural, instinctive, and expected reaction to loss. Initially, this definition may seem understated for the death of a child, but a better understanding of your grief lies within these simple words.

Your understanding of grief probably came from the losses you've faced in the past, for each loss generated some type of grief response within you, even if you weren't tuned into it. For example, the loss of a first cousin whom you saw only at family weddings and funerals may have brought on a fleeting moment of sadness when you thought of the fun you had together as kids. Was this sadness a moment of grief? Yes. How about your inability to concentrate after your brother died suddenly? Yes again. Your lack of concentration was part of your grief reaction to the loss of your brother.

Losing a child to death is a sorrow unlike any other.... Simply said, it is just plain wrong for your child to die before you.

Presumably, you've lived through other losses and some of them may have been deeply personal ones; nevertheless, they paled in comparison to the gut-wrenching loss of your son or daughter. None of your previous encounters with death and grief could have prepared you for this crushing blow. Losing a child to death is a sorrow unlike any other.

In an earlier paragraph, grief is described as a natural reaction to loss. But there's nothing natural about the disruption to the normal cycle of life that took your child away from you. Surviving parents can't comprehend how this could have happened. Simply said, it is just plain wrong for your child to die before you.

★

PARENT-TO-PARENT

"My first husband was killed in Vietnam, but losing my son is a thousand times worse."

GRIEF'S PERFECT STORM

Devastating losses can trigger volatile reactions. Consequently, a child's death has the power to unleash within you a formidable grief that has been described as raw, intense, and, at times, extreme.

This formidable grief is built upon the intersection of three very powerful forces:

- Your child's death.
- The likelihood that it was sudden and unexpected.

- The multifaceted elements that military service brings
  to death.

Standing alone, each one of these circumstances presents daunting challenges in grief; the point where they converge often creates the perfect storm of grief for many parents.

In *How to Go on Living when Someone You Love Dies,* psychologist Therese Rando states, "Parental grief is particularly intense. It is unusually complicated and has extraordinary up-and-down periods. It appears to be the most long-lasting grief of all."

This formidable grief is built upon the intersection of three very powerful forces.

It is a grief unlike any other. And it can be a frightening one.

GRIEF REACTIONS

The list of grief reactions for a parent is diverse and lengthy. It's impossible to list every reaction you may have felt—or are still feeling—because your grief is personal and complex, just like your relationship with your child. Because of the complicated nature of a parent's grief, reactions that may seem out of proportion with other losses may be seen as being within a normal range for surviving parents.

As a Gold Star parent grieving for a lost child, perhaps you:

- Feel you've failed as a parent.
- Yearn for your son all the time.
- Search for him in public.
- Want the DoD to call and say it has made a mistake.
- Expected your daughter home when the deployment ended.
- Miss her so much you're physically sick.
- Feel a part of you died with your child.
- Feel like you're going crazy.

- Have nightmares about your son.
- Are emotionally numb or detached from others, including your spouse.
- Suffer an intense pain of separation from your son.
- Ask God why He didn't take you instead.
- Want to hold someone or something accountable for your son's death.
- Endure profound feelings of anguish, sorrow, or pain.
- Are emotionally fragile.
- Believe you could have prevented your son's death.
- Feel guilty for being alive.
- Are easily overcome by emotion.
- Feel purposeless.
- Are relentlessly irritable, impatient, or intolerant.
- Feel angry at everyone and everything.
- Have dreams you son is leaving you.
- Are sometimes confused.
- Notice you sigh for no reason.
- Experience the need to do something strenuous or physical.
- Take attacks on America personally.
- Feel chronically sad.
- Are consumed by fatigue.
- Get sick more often.
- Think you no longer have control over anything.
- Feel anxious or agitated.
- Are restless, but with no place to go.
- Pace back and forth for no good reason.
- Are easily startled.
- Feel absentminded.
- Are bewildered and at times disoriented.
- Think your memory has stopped working.

- Are overwhelmed by making decisions.
- Can't think logically or, at times, rationally.
- Are stymied by simple tasks.

Every reaction listed here need not be present for you to feel the depth or the fullness of your grief. Likewise, you may have experienced others that are not on this list.

Understand that any intention to harm or kill yourself or another person is not a grief reaction.

Understand that any intention to harm or kill yourself or another person is *not* a grief reaction. If you feel you will harm or kill yourself or someone else and you're planning to do it, call the National Suicide Prevention Lifeline at 1-800-273-8255 or call 911 now. They are lifelines at times like this.

★

PARENT-TO-PARENT

"I hurt and I ache. Then I hurt and I ache more."

INTENSE REACTIONS

Intense grief reactions are generally the norm for a surviving parent, although nothing about them feels normal. In the previous section, you reviewed the long list of parental grief reactions. In all likelihood you haven't experienced each one, nor would anyone expect you to do so. That list is diverse and comprehensive. But there are two reactions—guilt and anger—that are common and even expected in a mother or father.

Guilt

Guilt is an expected and powerful emotional reaction to the death of a child. It occupies a sizable place within a parent's grief. You may feel guilty for all sorts of reasons; sometimes you even feel guilty without knowing why. As with any emotion, guilt comes in varying degrees of intensity and duration.

Surviving parents have been known to judge themselves by unrealistic standards. You may feel you had a lasting responsibility to protect your child, regardless of age, marital status, occupation, or location. As a result, you may view your son or daughter's death as a parental failure. The guilt this perceived role failure generates can be daunting. It has a tendency to distort past actions and events, yet it changes nothing. And, if left unchecked, guilt has a long shelf life.

No relationship is perfect, including the parent-child one. You may have expressed guilt over what you did or didn't do when your child was alive. "If only I could have paid for college, maybe she wouldn't have joined the military," whispered Sandra. With the US divorce rate hovering around 50 percent, a number of surviving parents lived apart from their child. "I wish I'd spent more time with my son," said Dave, "but my ex remarried and moved across the country, so I only got to see him once or twice a year." Not surprisingly, you may also feel guilt over the *small stuff* that happened in your child's lifetime—stuff that didn't matter until you revisited it in hindsight.

> *[Guilt] has a tendency to distort past actions and events, yet it changes nothing. And, if left unchecked, guilt has a long shelf life.*

Moms and dads almost always experience survival guilt—feeling guilty for being alive when their child is dead, regardless of the cause. You may believe—in some way, shape, or form—that you could have prevented the death from happening. "I should've talked my son out of joining the Marine Corps," said Calvin, "but he insisted on following in my footsteps. Maybe if he had joined another service branch, things would've turned out differently."

The guilt felt by surviving parents of children who died by suicide is known to be acutely intense. If your child completed suicide, you may feel guilty over what you perceive you did wrong in raising your son or daughter or what signs you may have missed in your child prior to the death.

It may be necessary to remind yourself again and again that suicides have multiple causes. No one person, circumstance, or situation can be the single cause of a suicide death. As hard as it may be to understand, you aren't responsible for the actions of your child. "After Martin's death," said Sam, "I felt totally responsible for not saving my son from himself. I know now that's not true, but I was operating on pure emotion. It had nothing to do with thinking rationally."

★

PARENT-TO-PARENT

"I want my son to be remembered for who he was and not for his last actions."

Everything in your life may seem colored by guilt. At times, you may feel a little guilty for the way you grieve for your son, wondering if you're doing it the wrong way. Are you failing at grief because others seem to be holding up better? Not at all. If you don't grieve every waking minute of the day, does it mean you didn't love your daughter enough? Not in the least. Are you grieving enough? Probably. Is it okay to take a break from grief and not feel bad about it? Absolutely.

If your child wasn't married, in all likelihood you and/or your spouse received the military's death benefit and the Servicemembers' Group Life Insurance (SGLI) program. Sometimes, just the thought of this money produces feelings of guilt.

You may feel it's blood money, the payoff for your son's life. You may also feel guilty for using it to improve your quality of life, such as paying off debt or buying a new house. Some parents feel guilty for spending it a little too quickly or frivolously, actions that happen more than you realize. It's easy to adopt a "life is short" attitude. After all, life *was* too short for your child.

You can expect guilt to be a part of your grief. Just like other emotions, grief requires you to face your guilty feelings and work through them. A good first step in resolving your guilt is to remember—and accept—that you're human. And even with the best of intentions, humans lead imperfect lives.

Anger

Anger is a universal component of grief and loss. Like guilt, it's often a powerful reaction to the loss of a child. You have every right to be angry; death stole your child away from you.

Anger has many disguises. It can masquerade as irritability or frustration, or that last little irritating action that sends you over the edge. Anger also comes in varying degrees of intensity, from smoldering resentment to blind rage. As with grief, the intensity of your anger depends on your relationship with your child and how the death happened. And, as with guilt, anger can have a long shelf life if not worked through.

Anger hunts for a target. If your son died from an illness, a disease, a genetic condition, or other natural cause, you may notice you're angry with a number of surprising sources. Perhaps you're angry with yourself or your spouse for passing a defective gene on to him. You may

You have every right to be angry; death stole your child away from you.

be angry with him for not reacting sooner to medical signs that something was amiss. Possibly, military medicine is the target of your anger for not detecting this lurking defect at an induction physical or for not treating your son more aggressively when this condition presented itself and eventually worsened. Conceivably, your anger may find its target in God for allowing this condition to progress to death.

If your son or daughter died a sudden and traumatic death, especially one caused by the actions of another or by your child's own hand, your anger very likely has increased and your list of targets has grown larger. It needs to claim a target and devour it.

★

PARENT-TO-PARENT

"I need to hold someone accountable."

In those situations where your child died because of the actions of another, your escalating anger is probably focused beyond yourself or your family members. Your anger may be focused on an *individual,* such as a superior in your son's direct chain of command or the individual directly responsible for the death. It may also be directed at an *organization*—for instance, your son's service branch, the Department of Defense, or a military contractor—or at the leadership of the government, starting with the president and congressional lawmakers. Anger doesn't recognize national boundaries, and it can reach across oceans and continents. If your son died in a war or other hostile action, your anger may be directed at leaders of another country or the unknown enemy in a foreign land who killed him.

If your son died by suicide, you may be angry with him for ending his life. You may discover you're angry that he didn't give you one last chance to help him. You may blame your spouse for the death and direct your anger that way. Perhaps you blame yourself and turn your anger inward. You may also target the Department of Defense, the Department of Veterans Affairs, or all who work with military members or veterans for not taking better care of your son. And you may also be angry with the world, for judging your son solely by his death.

Be mindful that anger likes to take over. Particularly with sudden deaths, it's not uncommon for surviving parents to obsessively hunt for more facts, determine who or what is to blame for their child's death, try to affix responsibility for it, and demand accountability, justice, payback, or punishment.

★

PARENT-TO-PARENT

"I sometimes resent my friends with their perfect families and perfect lives."

FACTORS THAT INFLUENCE YOUR GRIEF

Parental grief can be confusing. On one hand, it has universal elements such as the pain of separation, longing for your child, sorrow, anger, and guilt. On the other hand, it's a grief that's deeply personal and unique only to you. Both statements are true.

Grief's universal elements are transformed into your personal grief by who you are as a person, who you lost to death, and how that death occurred. You didn't come into parental grief with a blank slate of life experiences. No one does. The life you've lived shaped many of your reactions and responses. The following sections examine how your grief is personalized.

Loss of Your Son or Daughter

The loss of a son or daughter is a traumatic loss for a parent, as it causes a permanent separation from the child and violates the expected cycle of life. Other factors that shape your grief are your child's place within your family and the substance of your relationship with him or her. To help you better understand how your family structure and your relationship with your child

Grief's universal elements are transformed into your personal grief by who you are as a person, who you lost to death, and how that death occurred.

influenced your personal grief, think about how these questions apply to you and your grief.

- Was your son an only child? An only son?
- Were you a single parent, adoptive parent, or stepparent? Were you the primary parent?
- Was your daughter married? Did she have children?
- Were you close to your child? Or was your relationship strained or broken?

How Your Child Died

On top of the physical loss of your son or daughter, the circumstances of the death have a major effect upon your grief. All parents feel a profound level of pain when their child dies. But the type of death, its circumstances, and its suddenness all greatly contributed to how you initially reacted and what you have to contend with now and later in your grief.

- Was your son's death anticipated or unexpected? Random or intentional?
- Was your son killed? Did he die by suicide?
- Does your child's cause of death embarrass or stigmatize you?
- Were you with your daughter when she died? Did others die with her?
- Was your son or daughter's body recovered? Were you able to view it?

The two sets of questions presented above pertain to your child. The remaining questions focus on you. Your age, gender, personality, coping behaviors, and physical and emotional health are all parts of your personal grief. Your family, ethnicity, and spiritual beliefs on death also influence how you grieve. Last, the amount of support you have in working through your grief plays a part in how you handle it.

Your Age at the Time of Death

- Are you still raising children who need you?
- Do you have a job that you depend on for income?
- Is your life in a state of change because of divorce or the death of your spouse?
- Were you in the middle of a "midlife crisis" at the time your child died?
- Are you caring for elderly parents who depend on you?

Your Physical and Emotional Health

- Do you have a physical illness, disability, or disease that you're dealing with? A chronic or incurable condition?
- Are you dealing with depression, anxiety, or another mental health condition?
- Were you under significant amounts of stress before your child's death?
- Are there other crises happening in your life now?

Your Gender, Personality, and Coping Behaviors

- How did you react to previous deaths or traumatic events?
- Are you the one whom others depend on to be strong and keep it together?
- Do you think expressing grief is a sign of weakness?
- Is it uncomfortable to share your grief or seek out support in others?
- Do you use alcohol or other drugs as part of your coping mechanisms?

Your Family, Ethnicity, and Religious Beliefs

- Have you had recent deaths in your family?
- Is your family open about death or do they not talk about it?
- Within your cultural or ethnic background, what are acceptable behaviors after a death?
- How do your beliefs about life, death, and an afterlife influence you?

Your Support System

- Do you have someone you can trust?
- Have you sought out other parents with similar losses?
- Are you a part of a grief group, or are you seeing a counselor for your grief?

These last five sets of questions have hopefully guided you to a better understanding of how your personal grief is influenced by the person you are and the experiences you've lived.

LESSON LEARNED

The pain from the loss of a child is universal; your pain from the loss of your child is profoundly personal and unique to you.

SUMMING IT UP

The loss of a child to death produces a grief that is unlike any other. You share some of grief's universal elements with other parents who have lost a child, such as the pain of separation, longing for your child, anger, and guilt. Yet your grief is also personal and unmistakably influenced by the strength of your attachment to your son or daughter, the cause of death, how it happened, and your child's military service.

★

CHAPTER 7

Grief Is a
Package Deal

Our daughter, Nicole, was killed in a freak accident on base. She initially survived but was badly injured and died in the emergency room. Nicky's death has knocked the wind out of me, and I've become fixated on the circumstances that led up to it. It didn't have to happen. When you get right down to it, though, I guess all accidents are preventable in some way. My Nicky was just in the wrong place at the wrong time.

I've never lost a child and so I don't know what to expect. People tell me I'm holding up rather well—whatever that means. I nod my head in agreement because I don't know what to say.

The truth is, I think I've aged thirty years since my Nicky died. Everything I do is an effort these days. I'm always tired and feel like a slug most of the time. My wife says I've put on weight. My guess is around twenty-five pounds, but honestly, I don't care. I really don't understand how it happened because food doesn't taste too good anymore, except for that bottle of bourbon I have stashed away in the garage.

Now I feel like I have an ulcer. As much as I hate to say it, I need to see a doctor.

Jim (Kentucky)

As a speaker on military loss, I've sometimes asked audiences to describe grief. More often than not, they portray grief by describing visual emotional reactions, such as tears, the look of sorrow, and/or displays of anger. These are good answers, and all these reactions may be a part of grief. But they don't make up its complete description. That's because there are other components to grief. In addition to its emotional aspects, grief also has physical, behavioral, and cognitive components, as well as social and spiritual ones.

Grief is a package deal.

Unfortunately, you can't customize grief by picking and choosing your own components. Grief is a package deal.

INITIAL REACTIONS

In all likelihood you learned about your son or daughter's death through the casualty notification process of your child's service branch. This process is an undeniably unnerving one, starting with the presence of uniformed military personnel and the scripted formality of the death notification. Many moms and dads have described this notification process as surreal, especially because the purpose of it is to inform you that your child has died. Most likely, this news was unexpected, given that more than 80 percent of military deaths are sudden ones.

A sudden death, coupled with an unnerving casualty notification, can bring on a state of shock in surviving parents. This shock may have left you feeling stunned, in denial, and not able to piece together all you were told. Once the shock had subsided a bit, you may have become aware of other feelings and reactions. Most likely, your initial reactions were very intense, adding to the overall distress of this time.

There is a wide range of initial reactions that would be considered normal for surviving parents, but not all parents react in the same way, nor will every mother and father experience every reaction. It's impossible to list everything you've felt, but some of your immediate reactions to the news of your child's death may have included:

- Shock
- Denial
- Disbelief
- Uncertainty

- Numbness
- Unreality
- Helplessness
- Disconnectedness

★

PARENT-TO-PARENT

"I thought if I didn't talk to the military when they came, their news wouldn't be true."

EMOTIONAL REACTIONS

Emotional reactions are commonly recognized as a visible sign of grief, but they're only part of grief's total emotional package. For example, tears have a rightful place in grief, but aren't the only way to express emotions. Some parents aren't visibly emotive and don't show their feelings with tears. The emotional side of their grief may present itself in other ways, such as through irritability, anger, or yearning, to name just a few reactions. What is an appropriate emotional reaction for one parent may not even register with another.

What is an appropriate emotional reaction for one parent may not even register with another.

★

PARENT-TO-PARENT

"I cry without tears."

You can count on your emotional reactions to change from week to week, day to day, and, sometimes, hour to hour. Some reactions you may never experience a second time; others come back again and again. While there's no emotional checklist, here are a few emotional responses, in addition to those listed earlier under initial reactions that would be considered normal for a surviving parent:

- Disbelief
- Numbness
- Yearning
- Crying
- Helplessness
- Shame
- Irritability
- Sorrow
- Panic attacks

- Anger
- Depression
- Turmoil
- Guilt
- Fearfulness
- Anxiousness
- Emptiness
- Rejection
- Abandonment

BEHAVIORAL REACTIONS

Behaviors aren't normally thought of as a part of grief. However, they can be a powerful way that grief comes out for some parents. This side of grief can sometimes be misunderstood as bad behavior, particularly when the actions of some mothers or fathers can be viewed as out of place for a grieving parent.

[Behaviors] can be a powerful way that grief comes out for some parents.

Behaviors show up in your grief in all kinds of ways. At some point, you may be restless, feeling the urge to move or "do something," even if you don't know where you want to go or what to you want to do. Perhaps you've assumed a mannerism or two of your child, possibly not even realizing it until it was pointed out to you. How about developing a craving for your child's favorite food? In public, are you always on guard, alert to "seeing" your child in the hope of bringing him or her back into your life? All of these behaviors are part of your grief, especially early on. On some level, you're striving to keep your child close as the painful reality of the death sinks in.

Grief has been described as internalized chaos, somewhat akin to an active volcano. Sometimes it's too unsettling to even think about this chaos, much less want to put it into words. Some parents may act out their internalized chaos through a variety of positive or negative behaviors, often without realizing they're doing it.

Acting out can be positive when it's channeled into physical actions, such as manual labor, an all-consuming project, or a sport that uses a great amount of physical energy. It can also be as simple as beating up a pillow or two and releasing the pent-up anger, anxiety, or whatever emotion lies within you.

Engaging in any behavior with an "I don't care" attitude can be trouble.

Acting out can be negative when it displays itself in actions that are high risk, harmful, or destructive to yourself or others. For example, one possible area for acting out may be your driving habits. "I never thought of it as grief," remarked Marco, "but I've turned into an impatient madman behind the wheel."

Spousal abuse can also be a sign of acting out, as can any actions or behaviors that have the tendency to bring out the worst in you.

Increased or excessive alcohol use, chronic emotional overeating, abusing prescribed medications, or using illegal substances are also signs of negative behaviors. Engaging in any behavior with an "I don't care" attitude can be trouble.

Be open to listening when a family member or friend mentions that your behavior has changed. You may not be aware that you're acting or behaving differently. Here are some behavioral reactions that may—or may not—be a part of your grief. It's good to be aware of all of them:

- Searching
- Preoccupation
- Restlessness
- Pacing
- Acting out
- Assuming mannerisms
- Anxiousness
- Edginess

- Disturbing dreams and nightmares
- Apathy
- Agitation
- Neglect of appearance
- Disregard for personal hygiene
- Avoidance

PHYSICAL REACTIONS

Most people usually don't connect physical symptoms to grief. But physical responses can be a major component of grief. It's important to recognize and understand them in order to better cope with these reactions.

Grief is a powerful stressor. It can show up in unexpected places within your body.

Grief is a powerful stressor. It can show up in unexpected places within your body. Grief may weaken your immune system, causing you to get sick. Or a prior medical or mental health condition may flare up unexpectedly, even after years of being a nonissue.

Grief has a pesky habit of affecting your body in disturbing ways. Are you easily startled? Do you feel like you've aged since your child died? Do your back and neck constantly ache? Have you lost your appetite, or do you eat everything in sight? Has your sex drive changed? Do you shy away from sex to avoid finding pleasure or intimacy in it? Are you bone-tired, but unable to asleep? How about not wanting to get up and out of bed? Do you have flashbacks of a past trauma? Have you developed indigestion or other gastrointestinal changes that have left you out of sorts? Do you hear or see things that others do not? Do you sigh for no reason? Have you noticed that your asthma or allergies have flared up? Is something else bothering you physically or mentally? Grief isn't picky about what it affects.

The list of ways that grief physically affects a person can be as long as the number of surviving parents. Here is a partial list of physical reactions that surviving moms and dads have experienced:

- Dry mouth
- Sighing
- Tension
- Fatigue
- Illness
- Insomnia
- Back pain
- Headaches
- Palpitations
- Anxiety attacks
- Hallucinations
- Gastrointestinal distress
- Appetite changes
- Change in sexual desire and interest
- Altered sleep patterns
- Hair loss

It's important to talk about any physical changes you've noticed with a doctor or medical health professional. These noticeable changes can be a sign of a medical problem. Now isn't the time for self-diagnosis or taking a "so what?" attitude. While this attitude may be what you're feeling at the time, it's never a good idea to ignore your health. It is vital that you maintain your physical and emotional health now more than ever.

★

PARENT-TO-PARENT

"I'm an emotional eater."

It's also a good idea to get a physical after your child's death. You may be surprised at how grief has already affected you physically, even without you knowing it. A visit to your healthcare professional can identify any emerging health issues and nip them in the bud.

It's not a good idea to neglect your health. A new or chronic health condition can get in the way of grieving for your child.

COGNITIVE REACTIONS

While grief is affecting your emotions, behavior, and physical health, there's a good chance it's also disturbing your ability to think clearly, concentrate, or make decisions. It's common for survivors to feel as if

It's common for survivors to feel as if their brains have stopped working.

their brains have stopped working. Have you found that your ability to think things through seems to have slowed down? Do you read a paragraph and can't remember what you've just read? Has your memory stopped working? How hard is it to do simple tasks, such as following a recipe or adding two numbers together? Difficulty with any of these is considered normal with grief. Normal or not, having such difficulties can be frustrating, especially at a time when you don't need another burden placed upon you. Unfortunately, the world doesn't stop for grief and let you catch up.

★

PARENT-TO-PARENT

"I was petrified that I was getting Alzheimer's disease."

Grief's cognitive impact puts additional stress on you. You are not alone in feeling this way. Here are ways that some surviving moms and dads have experienced the cognitive side of grief:

- No concentration
- Loss of memory
- Slowed thinking
- Scattered thoughts
- No memory retention
- Forgetfulness
- Disorganization
- Easily distracted
- In denial
- Confusion
- No focus

The social reactions of grief may not be immediately obvious. There are few public role models of parental grief and, in all likelihood, you don't personally know another parent who has lost a child. You're on your own to figure out what to expect from interactions with your family, friends, and neighbors. You've been changed by the loss of your child, and how you interact with others—and how they interact with you—has changed, too.

You may have lost the desire to reach out to others. And you may feel that you don't have the motivation or energy to do so. Sometimes, the overwhelming nature of the loss of your child may cause you to withdraw.

You may have lost the desire to reach out to others.

If you do reach out, your reasons to contact family and friends will probably be different now. You may feel the need to get hold of those you feel safe with or seek the connectedness that comes from those you've known a long time. You may also want to talk about your child with people who knew your son or daughter throughout his or her life. You may also reach out for all of the practical reasons you did before your son or daughter's death.

Connecting with your family and friends may not go as you expect. Those who are closest may not know what to say or how to help out. In an attempt to help, they may try to fix your grief, which can come across as minimizing your loss. Some family and friends may be uncomfortable with your grief and find reasons to keep their distance. Likewise, parents who have never lost a child may unconsciously not want to be around a mom or dad whose child has died.

★

PARENT-TO-PARENT

"My grief isn't contagious. Where are my friends?"

Sometimes, the cause of your child's death makes people shy away, especially when the death is stigmatized by society, which can be the case with suicide, homicide, and self-inflicted accidents.

Your son or daughter's death likely increased your sensitivity level, which is understandable. And so, if you don't get the type of support you are looking for, especially from family or friends, you may easily feel left out or abandoned. These feelings may be another secondary loss stemming from the death of your child.

Another element of grief's social reactions can be the change in your interest in and enthusiasm for activities that you found enjoyable in the past. They may not hold any interest for you now. Perhaps you want to isolate yourself as much as possible and avoid the greater world. Or the opposite is true, and you want to be in the company of others and out of your house or apartment.

As with all the other components of grief, there's a wide range of what's considered normal for a surviving parent. You might identify with a number of these reactions:

- Abandonment
- Sensitivity
- Neediness
- Avoidance
- Isolation
- Judgment

- Stress on relationships
- Hyperactivity
- Vulnerability
- Lack of interest
- Stigmatization
- Identity change as a parent

SPIRITUAL REACTIONS

The spiritual side of grief is often a powerful one. The death of your child undoubtedly challenged your fundamental views on the rightness of the world. Ostensibly, many of your accepted beliefs about the goodness of life, its meaning, and its purpose have been shaken by your child's death. Your beliefs may no longer be trusted as true.

PARENT-TO-PARENT

"I'm a good person. Why did this happen?"

Spirituality means different things to different people. It can be a part of, or separate from, the religious beliefs you hold. For some mothers and fathers, spirituality may stand on its own as a way of making sense of the loss and finding meaning in the world again; for others it is an integrated part of their religious beliefs. However you define it, your child's death presumably launched you on a spiritual quest for answers to some of life's toughest questions:

Spirituality means different things to different people.

- Why my son or daughter?
- Why did my child die while bad people continue to live?
- Why did God ignore my prayers when I prayed for my child's safety?
- Was this karma for some bad thing my son did? My daughter did? Or worse, something I did?
- Was I not a good enough parent that my child was taken away from me?

These questions are just the tip of the iceberg in your spiritual search. In all likelihood, this search has also turned inward as you look for answers to a host of hard questions, such as:

- Was there meaning in my child's death?
- What was the purpose of my son or daughter's young life?
- Is there another meaning and purpose in my life?

There are no easy answers to any of these questions. However, your spiritual search can lead you down the path to finding answers that can provide you with some peace of mind and a greater understanding of life and of death.

The death of your child also may have challenged your personal view of God, a deity that nine out of ten Americans believe in, according to Gallup polls. This can be quite upsetting in the darkness of grief, especially when all that you've come to believe and trust has been rattled by your child's death.

It sometimes happens that grieving mothers and fathers distance themselves from the God they believe in. Some parents experience a crisis of faith after their child's death, while others find solid strength and comfort in God, their faith community, and their religious beliefs in life after death and reunion with their son or daughter. A number of surviving moms and dads fall somewhere in between.

Regardless of how much or how little faith you had when your child died, his or her death will likely propel you to examine your beliefs about the God you believe in, the relationship you have with Him, and the role He plays in your life. Just as with your search for answers to life's unanswerable questions, this examination can lead you to a deeper understanding of your God and more of the peace of mind you seek.

This spiritual search is an important one and shouldn't be minimized or skipped. It may take years—but it's worth it.

LESSON LEARNED

Grief is a package deal of emotional, behavioral, physical, cognitive, social, and spiritual reactions.

SUMMING IT UP

Remember that grief is a package deal; those physical, emotional, behavioral, cognitive, social, and spiritual reactions don't occur in any particular order. Sometimes you may experience multiple reactions together, with some more pronounced than others. At other times, one or two reactions may dominate how you feel. Unfortunately, you can't customize your grief by picking and choosing your reactions or the order or the time you experience them.

Nothing about grief is predictable. It is what it is.

CHAPTER 8

★

Grief Work after a Military Death

I sometimes wonder how I made it through those first few years after Zach's death. My husband and I didn't talk about our son as much as I wanted, and I felt stuck in our mundane conversations and unspoken pain. I tried a grief group, but I was the only military mom in the group and I couldn't relate to the others. And so I tried counseling. I was hesitant about seeing a counselor, but nothing else was working for me. Thankfully, I clicked with the first one I went to see.

I credit my counselor with saving my sanity. He says I saved my own sanity; he was merely the guide through the living hell of my grief.

My grief has changed over time, lessening in pain and intensity. Yet it still remains a part of me. However, now I can read a good book and remember the plot. I've discovered I enjoy repurposing furniture. And I've stopped scouring the obituaries for ninety-five- year-olds and wondering what made them so special to live that long.

Delores (Ohio)

The late Rose Kennedy has long been the recognized matriarch of the Kennedy political clan—a family that has had its share of tragedy and death. The mother of nine children, Rose Kennedy was no stranger to losing an adult child—or, in her case, several children. She is most recognized and remembered as the mother of President John Kennedy, who was assassinated in office in 1963, and Senator Robert Kennedy, who was also assassinated while running for president in 1968. These were not her only children to die suddenly and tragically. Rose Kennedy was also a Gold Star mother of World War II. Her oldest son Joseph, a Navy pilot in the war, was killed in action in 1944. Four years later, her daughter Kathleen, who was both married and widowed in World War II, was killed in a plane crash.

Rose Kennedy was the mother of nine children. Four of them were killed in sudden, traumatic ways.

TIME HEALS ALL WOUNDS?

This well-intentioned cliché is often dished out as hopeful and helpful advice to surviving parents. Undoubtedly, you would prefer to roll back time and rearrange the events on the day your child died. But that's not possible.

Speaking with the insight of a mother who lost four children, Rose Kennedy addressed the topic of time healing wounds. She has been quoted as saying, "It has been said that time heals all wounds. I don't agree. The wounds remain. Time—the mind, protecting its sanity—covers them with some scar tissue and the pain lessens, but it is never gone."

Usually called "grief work," it's a process of recognizing needs and taking actions that will help you to get through your pain and adjust to a life without your son or daughter.

GRIEF WORK

Time will not heal your wounds, but it can help reduce your pain by providing the opportunity to do the work that grief demands. What is the work of grief? Usually called "grief work," it's a process of recognizing needs and taking actions that will help you to get through your pain and adjust to a life without your son or daughter.

Grief work also can help you feel better about yourself and life again.

You may have read other materials on grief and probably came across several models for grief work. While each may be worded differently, the message is basically the same, as they all lay out similar actions and needs of grief. In this book, I've used the grief models of internationally respected psychologists, Alan Wolfelt and Therese Rando to explain the work that grief demands. They describe ways to work through your grief in simple, easy-to-understand terms. They are:

- Experience and internalize the reality that your child is dead.
- Allow yourself to feel the pain of your loss.
- Adjust to a different relationship with your child.
- Develop a new self-identity in life.
- Search for meaning.
- Be open to support in your grief.

NEEDS OF GRIEF

It's important to note that dealing with grief is hard work and takes active effort on your part—you won't be able to passively slide through it. It is work and it requires enormous amounts of physical, mental, and emotional energy. After all, your grief is the result of losing a child whom you love unconditionally. And as hard as it may be to understand at this time, working through your grief will bring a good measure of healing and relief.

Grief is hard work and takes active effort on your part— you won't be able to passively slide through it.

Experience and Internalize the Reality That Your Child Is Dead

An important, but difficult, need in your grief is to acknowledge and internalize that your child is dead. This is no easy task, and you may find your brain and heart are often in conflict. While your brain is grappling to comprehend this terrible news, your heart is in denial, disbelieving and protesting all that you've been told.

Initially, there's little connection between what you know intellectually and what you recognize emotionally. As every surviving mother and father knows, the reality of your child's death takes time to sink in. The emotional recognition that your child is dead is the

While your brain is grappling to comprehend this terrible news, your heart is in denial ...

first step; the emotional acceptance that your child is dead is much slower in coming. It is an ongoing process, often taking years.

The nature of many military deaths may hamper your early ability to acknowledge that your child is dead. In all probability, your child's death was a sudden one. He or she likely lived at a duty station, away from the home of record. The death may have occurred on deployment, a time when your child was supposed to be away. Your child's body may not have been viewable or even recoverable. And if your child was married, you weren't the primary next of kin and probably not the decision maker regarding how the remains would be handled, the type of funeral or memorial service held, or the final resting place of your child. All of these factors can get in the way of believing and internalizing that your son or daughter is dead.

★

PARENT-TO-PARENT

"I know my child is dead. I just don't like using the 'dead' word."

As you struggle with coming to grips with your child's death, you may experience varied and often intense reactions for some time. While some of these reactions may be uncomfortable, they're likely a natural and helpful part of your grief work.

For example, those feelings of helplessness may be your psyche's way of telling you that the death can't be "undone." Perhaps you feel compelled to tell the story of how your son died over and over. While those close to you may say not to dwell on it, retelling the story of his death is especially helpful in the early stages of your grief. Each time you tell the story, it becomes a little more real for you. Are you preoccupied with thoughts of your daughter? It's your heart and soul's way of holding onto her as the reality of the death sinks in. You may also have other reactions, many of which you read about earlier in this book. They're all a part of your grief work.

Allow Yourself to Feel the Pain of Your Loss

The feelings of love you had for your child didn't die with him or her. Because this love endures, the earthly loss of your son or daughter frequently ignites an excruciating pain and sorrow within and around you.

A part of your grief is to experience the pain and work through it. No parent would willingly embrace this type of pain. But the death of your son or daughter is the loss of your child's physical presence and also the loss of your exclusive parent-child relationship with him or her. These losses extract a great price from a parent.

Your pain reminds you that your child is dead and isn't coming back.

Your pain reminds you that your child is dead *and* isn't coming back. This physical separation is a permanent one.

You may experience this pain in many forms and through many reactions. In addition to the physical and emotional sides of your grief, a part of your personal pain may result from other strong feelings, such as parental failure, guilt, or shame. Likewise, feelings of depression, irritability, or anger that you may carry with you are a part of your grief—as are many other feelings you may experience. Know that your pain is made up of many expressed—and unexpressed—feelings and reactions.

PARENT-TO-PARENT

"There are days when I feel like a walking pincushion."

It may be hard to grasp, but experiencing the pain and working through it helps to heal your body, mind, and spirit. It inches you closer to a more manageable grief, one that is less intense and will not consume you day and night. Your progress through grief may not be immediately obvious to you because it's usually found in little things that sometimes go unnoticed in the moment.

There will come a time when you no longer count the months since your child died; you get through a day without crying; you genuinely laugh at something funny; you look forward to an event; or you wake up one morning and your son or daughter isn't your first waking thought. These events will happen one day, without warning or fanfare. And you may not realize their significance until after the fact. It's progress through grief.

When it comes to grief, it's pay now or pay later—you can count on grief to come back at a time and a place of its own choosing.

Grief work is vital to lessening your pain. And it's important to work through your pain and grief in non-self-destructive ways that best suit you. However, trying to avoid the pain will not make it go away—you can count on grief to come back at a time and a place of its own choosing.

Some years ago, then Marine Corps Chaplain Will Hood told me, "Don't put your energy into avoiding the pain. When it comes to grief, it's pay now or pay later." Chaplain Hood was right. And he spoke from his experiences as a military chaplain and the surviving father of a young son.

Doses of Reality

The reality that your child is dead comes in doses. Reality doesn't have sensitivity or good manners, and you may be confronted with a harsh dose when you least expect it. Likewise, reality seems to operate on its own arrival schedule.

Because of the public and private nature of your loss, you find reality in all kinds of settings, symbols, objects, and places. Sometimes reality comes from symbols of our country or national news events; other times reality shows up in your day-to-day life, in moments and circumstances that are understood only by you. Each time reality confronts you, it teaches you again that your child is dead. Over time and with grief work, these doses of reality will lessen in frequency and painfulness.

Each time reality confronts you, it teaches you again that your child is dead.

This list gives you an inkling of just a few ways that reality may bring you up short. Your list will probably be longer and definitely more personal to you.

- An old card in your son's handwriting.
- Fireworks on the Fourth of July.
- Your daughter's favorite potato chips.
- Your son's name on a headstone.
- The American flag.
- Your grandchildren calling another person "Mom" or "Dad."
- Any service member in uniform.
- Expired tags on your daughter's vehicle.
- News of other military deaths.
- Movies with military scenes.
- The melody of "Taps." Anytime. Anyplace.
- A New Year beginning without your son.
- A special song.
- Important days of meaning.

- Any and all holidays.
- A new phone number your daughter will never call.
- Dark chocolate brownies.
- The month/date of the death displayed on your digital clock twice a day.

Adjust to a Different Relationship with Your Child

Another part of your grief work is to convert the earthly relationship with your son or daughter to a relationship of memory or spirit. This is a challenge, for you have a lifetime of parental ties to your child, plus a built-in reluctance to give them up.

You will always have continuing bonds with your child, but death has changed the nature of them.

You will always have continuing bonds with your child, but death has changed the nature of them. An important need in your grief is to find a new place in your life for your child and new ways of relating to him or her. This is a very personal need and, unquestionably, a relationship that will be exclusive to you.

Remembering

One way to begin forming that changed relationship is through memories of your son or daughter, as well as shared memories from others who knew him or her. You know very well that stories about your child are priceless. Initially, these stories are bittersweet, but talking about your child is a part of grief. With time, stories and memories can make you feel good and help highlight the many different sides of your son or daughter.

It's a common tendency for many surviving parents to idealize their child in death, sometimes putting that child on the fast track to sainthood. While this is easy to do, it can shortchange your grief work because you're not remembering the real son or daughter. It's important that your memories of your child be realistic ones. Remember the real son or daughter, warts and all. That's the child you grieve for.

"My son was quite a handful growing up," recounted Brenda. "As a baby, Tyler had his days and nights mixed up. When he was awake, all he did was cry and scream. He was such a terror in grade school, always into some sort of trouble. I think I spent as much time in the guidance counselor's office as Tyler did. High school was a nightmare. Tyler thought rules didn't apply to him. With his attitude, I was dumbstruck when he wanted to join the military right after high school. To be honest, I was relieved the Army wanted Tyler, because he'd be out of my hair and my house for a while. I had high hopes the military would have better luck making him grow up than I did." Then Brenda whispered, "Now, I'm eaten up with guilt for feeling that way."

Most surviving mothers and fathers fear their son or daughter will be forgotten. And so, in all likelihood, you will become the keeper of your child's memory.

Most surviving mothers and fathers fear their son or daughter will be forgotten. And so, in all likelihood, you will become the keeper of your child's memory. And you'll work to keep that memory alive in many ways. The possibilities are endless.

Remembering the good old days is a part of your grief. You'll strive to remember everything you can about your child, beginning with the earliest days. Personal objects belonging to your child—such as pictures, cards, report cards, clothing, toys, and many more items—become irreplaceable.

These keepsakes have a sentimental history and become precious links to your son or daughter in a deeply personal way. Sometimes called "linking objects," these items keep you connected with your child. However, not every linking object comes from your son or daughter's past. You may maintain a connection to your child by wearing a military ball cap, a sports team sweatshirt, a gold star, or a piece of jewelry with personal meaning, to name just a few ways.

If your child was married, his or her personal effects belong to the surviving spouse. You may or may not have had access to those last personal possessions, some of which may have been with your child when death occurred. It's unfortunate if you didn't get any personal possessions, especially anything that was a part of those last moments. These personal effects have particular significance because they share the final moments of your child's life. The lack of these last personal possessions may be a significant secondary loss for you.

★

PARENT-TO-PARENT
"I put my son's old T-shirt into a big plastic bag because it still smelled like him."

Memories may also be public ones. Some service members have public displays of remembrance—a dedicated building, street, or memorial, for example—and these serve to ensure that the service member's memory will not fade away, though this isn't the case for the majority of our deceased service members. However, the spirit, service, and sacrifice of all the fallen are remembered in ceremonies across the country on Memorial Day. And, at least for one day, deceased service members aren't forgotten.

Sometimes you may unconsciously stay connected to your child by adopting some of his or her personal phrases, habits, or likes and dislikes. "Angela was crazy about blackberry jam, and so we always kept a jar in the refrigerator," recalled Ruby, "just for those times when she'd be home. After our Angie took her own life, my husband Paul developed a craving for blackberry jam. I was in too much of a fog to notice much, but I vaguely remember that Paul put Angie's jam on everything he ate, including his green beans."

Other Children

Referring to your lost child as your favorite or idealizing him or her may have some unintended consequences. For example, if you have other children, repeatedly hearing that their sibling was the favorite may deeply hurt their feelings or make them feel unloved. A military death and the sibling grief that follows are hard on brothers and sisters, too. With attention given to you and your spouse, and/or your child's surviving spouse, the grief of your other children may go unnoticed and their needs can easily be overlooked.

It is also important to remember that your other children face multiple losses with the death of their brother or sister. Not only did they lose a sibling, but they also lost their "old" mother and father...

It is also important to remember that your other children face multiple losses with the death of their brother or sister. Not only did they lose a sibling, but they also lost their "old" mother and father, the old you who existed beforehand.

Converting your relationship to one of memory or spirit is a slow process. And it hurts to do so. Yet in working through the pain, you begin to let go of it, making room to remember your child with love, warmth, and comfort.

Letting go of your pain and sorrow doesn't mean you're letting go of your child.

Letting go of your pain and sorrow doesn't mean you're letting go of your child. It simply means there is now some room in your heart and soul for the new relationship with him or her.

Develop a New Self-Identity

Your child's death robs you of many things, one of which is the old you. Your identity as a parent and possibly as a person is shattered by your child's death. You've been changed by it. You're not the same person you were beforehand. How could you be?

★

PARENT-TO-PARENT

"Yesterday I was an Army Mom. Who am I today?"

Your personal identity may be lost for a time. It's easy for grief to smother who you are, especially during the hardest times of internalizing your loss and working through the pain. And because your son or daughter donned the uniform, your grief is shrouded in America's flag. The death of your child forced upon you an identity you never wanted and one you may have feared—that of a Gold Star parent.

Who Are You Now?

Because of the magnitude of military loss, you may see yourself solely as a grieving mother or father of a deceased service member. Initially, this public identity may serve many purposes. It is a way of keeping your son or daughter close to you, especially as you internalize your child's death and contend with its intense grief. It also joins you with your child's commitment to the military because you now live with his or her death as a consequence of that commitment.

Additionally, this public identity as a Gold Star parent may aid in keeping your child's memory and spirit alive, such as on occasions where you're introduced as the surviving parent of a fallen service member or when you incorporate your loss into a personal conversation. And it may bring about continued support through offerings of condolence and thanks from caring strangers who learn of your story.

This public identity as a Gold Star parent can also have its downsides. It may keep you in an acute grief mode for too long a time, as it necessitates that you focus only on your son or daughter's death, often overshadowing the many sides of your child's personality and life. It also can cause you to slow down your journey through grief, delaying your progress on working through your pain and letting go of it.

A challenge as a Gold Star parent is to not let this public identity become your only one....as the old you was swept away, a new you is developing, one who was thrust into a world of living hell— and survives.

A challenge as a Gold Star parent is to not let this public identity become your only one. Try not to let the other parts of who you are slip away or seem less important. You will always be a surviving military parent *and* you are so much more. Remember that a part of you remains a spouse, a parent to other children, a daughter or son in your own right, and a warm, gifted, and courageous woman or man. And there are more roles and qualities that make up who you are.

In the hardest times of your grief, you may feel that you've lost a sense of who you are. It's common for moms and dads to feel this way. But, as the old you was swept away, a new you is developing, one who was thrust into a world of living hell—and survives.

As you work to survive, cope, and adjust to your child's death in the months and years to come, you'll rely upon personal skills that you've developed over a lifetime, as well as new ways of coping and adapting. You'll likely change and grow on your grief journey. In the midst of it, though, these changes may not be obvious. This will come down the road.

Growth after a Traumatic Loss

Psychologists Richard Tedeschi, PhD, and Lawrence Calhoun, PhD, have studied individuals who have lost a loved one, and they have found that people may experience personal growth as a result of their struggle through grief. Coining the term "posttraumatic growth," Tedeschi and Calhoun found that men and women who have experienced a major life crisis or traumatic event, such as the death of a child, noticed positive changes and growth in themselves because of their struggle with loss and grief.

As with everything else in grief, not every mother or father will undergo this growth to the same degree. In fact, it's possible that some parents will not undergo any growth at all. Grief can be peculiar like that.

In all likelihood, you'll grow and change in some ways as you do the work that grief demands. This growth, however, doesn't necessarily mean your suffering will lessen as you work through your grief. Changes and growth are usually noticed in hindsight. But the odds are in your favor that at some point in your grief journey you'll look back and see how far you've come and how much you've changed along the way.

Some changes you may notice are:

- Strengthened or closer relationships with family members or friends.
- A newfound or greater compassion, especially for other surviving families.
- An increase in personal resilience and inner strength.
- Greater sense of self-reliance and assertiveness.
- The ability to handle other traumatic situations.
- Less stress over the small stuff.
- A greater appreciation for life.
- A change in your philosophy of life.
- A change in priorities.
- A stronger faith.

★

PARENT-TO-PARENT

"I've survived the death of my child. I can handle anything."

Search for Meaning

Undoubtedly, the death of your son or daughter flies in the face of all you believe about how life should unfold. You're learning the hard way that life isn't fair, fate is fickle, and good men and women die young. After all, with your understanding of life already shaken, a key need in your grief is to strive to make meaning of your child's short life and death. Within this need, you'll fight through the unfairness of the death and attempt to make sense of it all. You will probably start with the

> *You're learning the hard way that life isn't fair, fate is fickle, and good men and women die young.*

cause of your child's death, attempting to clearly understand the events and circumstances that led up to it. You won't find all the answers you want—there's *never* enough information when it's your son or daughter. But your search for understanding is an important part of the need to make meaning of your child's life.

Service members die—or are killed—in many ways. When the death makes no sense, it's a struggle to find meaning in it. In these cases, surviving mothers or fathers often look to the bigger picture of military service to put their child's life into perspective. They find meaning and purpose in his or her service to America and in the promise to protect and defend it. At this time in our nation's history, that's a bold and courageous commitment, especially as bad guys actively plot to do great harm to America.

Personally speaking, I became a Gold Star widow when my young husband's helicopter exploded in midair on a training mission. My search for meaning in my husband Ken's death was a long and painful one, lasting many years. Eventually, I concluded there was no greater meaning in his death; but I found renewed meaning in Ken's short life. With laughing brown eyes and an all-American smile, Ken was simply one of the good guys. He loved his family, loved his country, and he loved to fly military helicopters. What more did I need to search for? Ken just ended up on the wrong side of that fine line between life and death.

Meaning in Your Life

In looking to make meaning of your child's life, you may begin to reexamine your own as well. Usually this doesn't happen early on in grief when survival and coping are your highest priorities.

Loss and grief have a way of rearranging life's priorities. When you eventually ask yourself the hard questions of who you are and where you're headed, you may notice that your priorities have changed. You've probably reordered what's important to you now—and what isn't. You see life differently. Finding answers to the questions of who you are now and what you're going to do will not happen right away. Answers of great importance take time.

Loss and grief have a way of rearranging life's priorities. It's sometimes the case that survivors want a greater good to come out of their profound loss. For some surviving parents, this desire puts their grief into action. There are many motivations and reasons to do so. And, as with so many aspects of grief, the reasons and level of commitment will evolve with time. Here's a sampling of motivations:

- Giving back to all who reached out in a time of need.
- Creating a better world for your grandchildren.
- Being an example of survival for the newest parents who walk in your shoes.

- Making a difference in an area that's important to you or your child.
- Becoming your best self, in spite of this life-changing loss.

It's an ongoing process to figure out the big questions of meaning and purpose after the death of your child. But it's worth it. It may lead you to a greater peace of mind, easing the hurt in your heart, mind, and soul in the process. It can also lead to discovering another purpose in your life. Loss and grief don't have to be the end of your story.

Loss and grief don't have to be the end of your story.

Be Open to Looking for Support in Your Grief

Without a doubt, the day has already come when you've asked, "Am I going crazy?" That's a normal and expected question, and odds are you'll ask it more than once. After all, you've been thrown into a world where your worst fear became real, and everything in your life that once was called normal has disappeared.

You know all too well that surviving the death of your military son or daughter is complex, complicated, and messy. You've lost your child *and* a military member. In many ways and on many levels, this double loss is isolating, for you experience a dual grief that few understand. But your grief doesn't have to be a solitary journey. And it can be hard to "fix" grief on your own. Be open to looking for support. It's available from many sources and in a variety of ways. In fact, you've already sought out support by reading this book.

Surviving mothers and fathers grieve in many different ways, so it's important to find the kinds of support that best suit you. What may be helpful for one parent may not even register with another.

National Organizations

There are two veterans' service organizations that provide support and resources to surviving military parents: the Tragedy Assistance Program for Survivors (TAPS) and the American Gold Star Mothers, Inc.

- **TAPS.** TAPS is the go-to organization for all who have lost a loved one in our armed forces. Within TAPS, you'll connect with other surviving mothers and fathers who *get it*, and you'll probably have much in common with them. TAPS offers an extensive variety of resources on a national, local, and personal basis, as well as online resources in an assortment of formats. To learn more about TAPS, go to www.taps.com or call their military survivor helpline at 800-959-TAPS.

- **American Gold Star Mothers.** American Gold Star Mothers offers local and national support for mothers whose sons or daughters have died on active duty, are missing in action, or died as a result of military service. American Gold Star Mothers provides understanding and encouragement to members through local chapters. They honor their fallen sons and daughters through service projects to aid wounded warriors, veterans, and their families who are in need. Learn more about American Gold Star Mothers at www.goldstarmoms.com.

- **The Compassionate Friends.** The Compassionate Friends (TCF) is a civilian organization and resource for mothers and fathers who have lost a child to any type of death at any age. They provide local, national, and online support to surviving parents who have lost a child. For more information on resources, check out www.compassionatefriends.org.

Online Grief Support

The internet is a treasure trove of information and resources on grief. There are online opportunities to connect with other military survivors through support groups, online chats, blogs, or other social media outlets. These resources connect you with other surviving mothers and fathers, giving you access to a national online community that shares the loss of a service member.

In addition, there is a host of information online about grief in general, and also the particular type of grief you may be contending with. On top of the loss of your service member, you may be dealing with the grief of losing your only child or the grief of a stepparent, for example. With a little searching, you can find credible, professional information on most types of grief.

The internet also provides you with a library of grief books, articles, and journals. The chance to read book reviews online is a great way to learn more about the content and readability of a book before you buy it.

Individual Support

Sometimes mothers and fathers are uncomfortable with seeking out professional support and may balk if counseling is suggested to them. But instead of wondering, "Do I need counseling?" a better question to ask is, "What can counseling do for me?"

… instead of wondering, "Do I need counseling?" a better question to ask is, "What can counseling do for me?"

A grief counselor can guide you in working through your grief in ways that are beneficial and supportive. In addition to being a great sounding board, the counselor can lend a hand when grief's irritating obstacles pop up along the way. And a grief counselor can help you develop the coping skills to live with the loss of your child in the years to come.

It is okay to ask a counselor about his or her experience with grief, particularly with the multifaceted elements of military grief and the loss of an adult child. You may even want to use this book as a guide as you work with your counselor. If you find you aren't comfortable with your counselor, it's also okay to ask him or her for a referral to another individual.

It's not too hard to find a grief counselor. Bereavement counseling is offered by the Department of Veterans Affairs at vet centers across America. You can also ask around, starting with your healthcare provider, your faith community, and, if you're comfortable, with family and friends. TAPS can also help in finding a counselor in your community.

Another way to find grief support is through structured grief groups or support groups. Both types of groups can be found locally. Structured grief groups usually have a firm start and end date and meet a set number of times. There is a group facilitator and usually a format to follow at each meeting. Support groups are usually open-ended, and an individual can join at any time. There is less structure to these groups, and topics may come from within the group or from the group leader.

LESSON LEARNED

Grief work helps to heal your body, mind, and spirit.

SUMMING IT UP

It's been said that grief is the price you pay for love. Because your love for your child is limitless, your grief may feel limitless, too. Early on, it may seem as though your pain will never lessen. But that's not the case. The best way to ease your pain is to put an honest effort into the needs of grief that were laid out in this chapter. And it helps to have the support of others along the way.

In working through your grief, you will probably come to realize that you're in a better emotional, physical, and spiritual place. Most likely, you'll find that your pain has lessened, your grief is becoming more manageable, memories of your child bring comfort rather than sorrow, you've found some peace of mind, and you've even discovered a little enjoyment in life again. Slowly and surely, you are healing.

Part Four

★

Coping

CHAPTER 9

Men and Grief

I was never one to wear my emotions on my sleeve, and I'm not going to start now. Just because I don't want to talk about how bad I feel doesn't mean that I'm not hurting. I miss Danny more than words can say. My son is never far from my thoughts and is forever in my heart. But I don't want to talk about it day in and day out. What good would it do? It won't bring Danny back.

I'll admit that grief sometimes gets the best of me. But that's my private matter and I don't need to share it with the world. I find it's worse at night. There have been nights when my thoughts and dreams all run together, and when I wake up, I'm not sure what's real.

I know my wife is hurting, yet I'm at a loss for finding ways to help her. I've struck out in just about every attempt I've made. I'm a little ashamed to say this, but sometimes I'm uncomfortable with her intense grief. At those times, I usually find something else to do and leave her alone.

Kenny (Virginia)

A child's death deeply wounds both parents. Yet how a father contends with the death and the grief that follows may bear little resemblance to the reactions of a mother. In the worst of times, death can magnify the differences in how men and women handle death and grief. And the world may not have a kind or tolerant view of a father's approach to grief.

Over time, our society—which includes families as well as faith and ethnic communities—has formed opinions on the "right way" for men and women to grieve. These opinions evolved into unwritten rules, defining what acceptable grief is for men and women. All too often this creates a problem for many men.

... when it comes to grief, men often end up with the short end of the stick.

America's perception of grief seems to follow the traditional model of grief usually identified with women, that is, one of visible and vocalized emotion. While this perception creates acknowledgment and sympathy for many visibly grieving mothers, it can disenfranchise grieving fathers who may express their grief in other ways. Consequently, when it comes to grief, men often end up with the short end of the stick.

Earlier in this book, the factors that shape individual grief and define military grief were laid out. Here, several more factors that play a role in defining grief for men will be tackled.

SOCIAL CONDITIONING

From the time they are born, babies are conditioned into gender roles. This helps them develop into who they are and how they behave as they grow into boys and girls and later into men and women.

Conditioning shapes expectations for a lifetime, both in how society perceives a man and in how this man sees himself. For example, little boys are told, "Big boys don't cry" and begin learning to keep their emotions in check. Likewise, "Don't be a sissy" teaches a boy to be strong, just as "Walk your little sister home from the bus stop" not only confers responsibility to bring his sister safely home, but also teaches the lesson that boys are protectors.

As a youngster, you were taught how to be a good boy. You carried these behaviors into adulthood and they probably have served you well. However, these learned behaviors were unquestionably tested by the death of your son or daughter.

... you may have thought any visible emotion on your part was a sign of weakness.

When your child died, it was probably next to impossible to keep your emotions fully in check. That emotional onslaught is too hard for most men to control—and it's not a good idea to do so. Since you learned emotional control as a youngster, you may have thought any visible emotion on your part was a sign of weakness. After all, you learned at an early age that big boys don't cry.

★

PARENT-TO-PARENT

"The men in my family don't cry."

In all likelihood, feelings of personal weakness are uncomfortable for you, especially when those feelings are trumped by traumatic grief. And just the thought of personal weakness can lead to thoughts of personal failure. "I feel like a failure because I couldn't protect Matt from death," said Joe, "and then I lost it in public. I feel guilty for letting my son down and for not being strong for my family."

It is normal to feel this way. In Joe's case, he's had a lifetime of conditioning that has shaped who he is and how he responds.

STEREOTYPES

Social conditioning and stereotypes go hand in hand. Good boys grow into men, learning as they grow to be problem solvers, providers, and protectors. These attributes serve them well as breadwinners, husbands, and fathers. Men value self-reliance and resiliency—every family should have a Rock of Gibraltar.

For many people, perception is reality. And our American stereotype of men is generally one of being the strong and silent type. In our society, men should be stoic and somber, yet sensitive and supportive to those around them.

Visible grief in men makes many Americans uncomfortable. It is often hard to figure out society's mixed messages about men and grief. On one hand, society anticipates men will remain composed in public. Limited emotion is tolerated, as long as it's modest and passes quickly. Visible grief in men makes many Americans uncomfortable. On the other hand, society can easily misread a man's controlled emotions as a lack of love and attachment for his child. This can lead to limited recognition of his loss and support for him, now and in the future.

As a father, you've probably walked a fine line in public between being strong for your family, keeping your composure, and grieving for your child. Even though society may have accepted that fleeting crack in your voice or those tear-filled eyes, you may have personally judged these actions as losing emotional control. While you may be your family's Rock of Gibraltar, the death of a child shakes the most resilient of men.

★

PARENT-TO-PARENT

"It was wearing me out to be strong all the time."

A LOSE-LOSE PREDICAMENT

In wrestling with grief, you may have found yourself in a lose-lose predicament. After a lifetime of your perfecting emotional control, your family, friends, and even some healthcare professionals probably expect you to grieve in precisely the opposite way. Our society still perceives grief as emotional reactions, ones that are displayed, verbalized, and shared. Few realize that emotions are only one way to experience grief. For some men and women, strongly displayed emotions are not how they respond to tragedy and loss.

When grieving differences aren't fully understood, one spouse's path through grief may be the other spouse's nightmare.

"I sometimes felt I was judged on how I did—or didn't—act," remarked Steven. "Why did it matter if I wanted to get back into my routine? I know my son is dead. I'm not ignoring that fact because I wanted to watch a football game with a couple of guys."

When grieving differences aren't fully understood, one spouse's path through grief may be the other spouse's nightmare. Mothers and fathers generally handle their child's death and the grief that follows in differing ways. Both are correct.

"I went to a grief group," said Dwight, "but didn't say much. I left because I got tired of hearing that I needed to 'let it all out.' That's not why I went in the first place. I just wanted to be around other parents who lost a child."

GENDERLESS GRIEF

Noted sociologist Ken Doka, PhD, and psychologist Terry Martin, PhD, initially set out to learn more about men and grief. In their research, they found patterns of grief reactions that could not be exclusively recognized as male or female traits. These patterns, which Doka and Martin called intuitive and instrumental grief, crossed over the male-versus-female grief divide.

INTUITIVE GRIEF

Intuitive grievers experience grief as feelings. Their inner pain is revealed through their visible emotions and actions. Feelings dominate their grief, and they're often intense and overwhelming. Crying and observable sorrow are common. Intuitive grievers genuinely need to experience and talk about their grief. To them, that's real grief.

Intuitive grievers experience grief as feelings. Their inner pain is revealed through their visible emotions and actions.

If you identify with intuitive grief reactions, you probably find comfort and strength in sharing your grief, especially with other surviving parents who have lost a child in military service. Because you use so much energy on emotions, you may often become exhausted, leaving yourself with little energy for other needs, such as taking care of yourself or your family.

INSTRUMENTAL GRIEF

Instrumental grievers also experience the inner pain of grief, but their reactions usually differ from those of intuitive grievers. They likewise contend with a range of feelings and emotions, but strive to keep them under control. Instrumental grievers may respond to feelings by redirecting that emotional energy into actions. They prefer not to talk about their feelings, but may gravitate to issues brought on by the loss and work to resolve them. They like to solve problems. When instrumental grievers are not taking action, they're most comfortable handling grief intellectually, tending to think their way through it.

Instrumental grievers also experience the inner pain of grief, but strive to keep them under control.

If you identify with instrumental grief, you probably experience a range of grief reactions, but the intensity or duration of these reactions may be less than those of intuitive grievers. You probably work to control your emotions, and may be uncomfortable around those who are openly emotional. You take action to work through your grief and may put your problem-solving skills to good use, perhaps by trying to restore order to the turmoil caused by the death.

MORE THAN ONE WAY TO GRIEVE

Doka and Martin showed that individuals do grieve in noticeably different ways, and there is no right or wrong way to get through it. They also determined that few people are exclusively either intuitive grievers or instrumental ones. Most men and women are blended grievers, experiencing both intuitive and instrumental reactions. Usually, though, a person will be more comfortable with one set of behaviors or the other, even though both may be present in his or her grief. Neither grief pattern is better than the other one.

MEN AND GRIEF

You'll emerge from grief a different man. In the meantime, being a Gold Star father puts you in a tough spot.

Chapter Six explained how the three powerful circumstances of military loss—your child's death, the likelihood it was sudden and unexpected, and the elements that military service bring to death—created the perfect storm of military grief.

You'll emerge from grief a different man.

With this perfect storm in play early on, you undoubtedly battled with the raw grief of your child's death, the bundle of unknown reactions it brings out, and your attempt to keep it together.

In the midst of this struggle, you've probably come up against the deep-rooted belief that genuine grief should be emotionally expressed. Consequently, while professionals and grievers alike may say that everyone grieves differently, you've probably been expected to grieve "like a woman."

Remember that grief is a package deal. It's made up of that intricate web of physical, cognitive, spiritual, behavioral, emotional, and social reactions that you read about in Chapter Six. Initially, grief has many unknowns. But as you experience and learn more about it, your personal style of grief emerges.

... while professionals and grievers alike may say that everyone grieves differently, you've probably been expected to grieve "like a woman."

A number of men identify with instrumental grief. If you do, you may recognize many behavioral or cognitive actions that are a part of your grief. Be mindful, though, that you may also wrestle with grief's emotional reactions at the same time.

At times, your grief may remind you of a sliding scale, with a number of reactions that can easily change in intensity with the situation. It's all part of that package deal. Nothing about grief is ever black or white.

COMMUNICATION

Grief can strain communication in marriages, causing added stress for grieving parents, each of whom is struggling with the shared loss of their child plus their own private grief. All too often, a couple's attempt to talk about their personal grief and its impact on each of them is compounded by the depth of their own grief, their comfort level in talking about it, and the heightened sensitivity brought on by their child's death.

It's a natural instinct to help others in ways you find helpful, even though it may not always be the best way to help out.

For instance, with the best of intentions, John suggested ways for his wife Jean to keep busy, as a way of getting her mind off things for a time. While staying busy worked for him, Jean saw his suggestion as avoiding grief rather than facing it. Likewise, when Jean asked John to talk about grief, she saw it as a loving and helpful gesture. John thought it was terrifying. When the conversation didn't unfold as she expected, Jean felt her help wasn't taken to heart and John wasn't grieving in the right way.

★

Keep in mind that the need to communicate with your spouse is a priority for your marriage. Now more than ever, talking with your spouse about the hard subjects of your child's death and how it affects you can help to avoid mistaken perceptions, misinterpreted actions, and unfulfilled needs for each of you.

LENGTH OF GRIEF

You can count on grief to stick around for quite a while. In all likelihood, it will take longer than

Grief has no respect for progress.

you'd like to work through the toughest parts of your grief. But don't be fooled into thinking that once the intensity of it lessens, you're finished grieving. It doesn't work that way. Grief doesn't unfold in an orderly or predictable way, and you may find that you've revisited issues and reactions time and again. It doesn't mean you're failing at it. Grief has no respect for progress. This unpredictability is a normal part of the process.

Psychologist Alan Wolfelt has often said that grief usually hurts more before it hurts less. Wolfelt's meaning can be seen in your grief work:

- It is heartbreaking to face the reality that your child is dead and feel that pain in its many forms.
- It hurts to accept that your earthly relationship with your child has ended, replaced by one of memory or spirit.
- It is tough to search for meaning in your child's short life and death and, perhaps, in your own life as well.

- It is sometimes difficult to look for help or support in
  your grief.

While these needs of grief are painful and exhausting,
experiencing the pain and working through it helps to heal your
body, mind, and spirit.

While these needs of grief are painful and exhausting, experiencing the pain and working through it helps to heal your body, mind, and spirit.

Your intense grief won't last forever. As you work through it, you'll notice it evolves and changes into something more manageable, one that doesn't consume you day and night. Yet some level of grief will remain with you. Without question, you'll spend the rest of your days adjusting to a life without your son or daughter.

TIPS FOR SURVIVING FATHERS

Many men like lists, probably because they organize things to do and plot a course of action. Regrettably, grief doesn't have an official checklist. However, here are ten tips you can use to help manage your journey through grief—it's the closest thing to a checklist for surviving military fathers:

1. **Learn about military loss, male grief, and the death of an adult child.** Thomas Jefferson wrote, "Knowledge is understanding." Especially now, understanding what you're experiencing is critical. Find out all you can about your specific type of grief and loss. Likewise, delve into what makes up your personal grieving style. This knowledge can provide helpful insight to meet your grief head-on.

2. **Anticipate an upheaval of body, mind, and spirit.** Grief feels strange. It's like no other force in life, especially the difficult grief

brought on by your child's death. You can expect a wide range of formidable reactions, which are generally a normal part of a parent's grief. Try not to minimize or dismiss your reactions, but recognize them for what they are: reactions to the death of your son or daughter.

3. **Participate in your healing by doing the work that grief demands.** The best way to work through grief is to face it head-on. Avoiding grief just guarantees problems down the road. Explore the needs of grief work. Give yourself plenty of time to strengthen your resolve and heal your body, mind, and spirit.

4. **Take on grief the way you've handled other tragedies.** Many men cope with death the same way they have responded to other tragedies in life. Be proactive on your grief journey to the best of your ability. Tap into the successful survival skills you've gained in life and be open to learning new skills. It's okay to ask for directions through grief.

5. **Watch out for harmful behaviors.** Drinking too much alcohol, abusing prescription medications, or using illegal substances to dull your pain is never a good idea. You'll probably regret it afterward. These substances can further cloud your already compromised ability to think clearly. In grief, participating in any behavior with an "I don't care" attitude can be trouble. Who needs more trouble?

6. **Don't ignore feelings of depression, anxiety, or not wanting to live.** Feelings of depression, anxiety, or not wanting to live are not uncommon after a traumatic loss. But don't ignore them or hope they'll improve on their own. Professional help is readily and confidentially available, and seeking out such

assistance is nothing to be ashamed of or embarrassed about. More men than you may realize have sought help and have been able to improve their mood and outlook.

There's a big difference between sometimes not wanting to live and thinking about ways to die. If you're thinking about suicide, call the National Suicide Prevention Lifeline now: 1-800-273-8255.

7. **Get moving.** Physical activity is good for you, whether it's exercise, labor, or a good old-fashioned walk outdoors. Physical activity can help relieve stress, improve your mood, and put your pent-up restlessness into action. Getting active may also be a way to work through some of your grief. And you may feel good after a little physical activity.

8. **Take a break from grief.** Hobbies, sports, and outside interests are good for surviving fathers. Putting attention, effort, and time into a personally rewarding project is an emotional battery charger. It also gives you permission to take a break from grief. Choose a project or interest that's not related to the military or other Gold Star families. It's okay to step away from military or Gold Star activities and do something for yourself or your family.

9. **Set boundaries with family and friends if necessary.** Your child's death altered your comfort zone. Sometimes it may be necessary to draw the line with others, regardless of their intentions. It's okay to set boundaries. Learn to recognize your hot buttons and aim to keep your distance from people, places, and things that push them.

10. **Seek out other fathers who have lost a child in the military.**
Connecting with other Gold Star fathers is often beneficial. With them, you'll find an unspoken bond that few understand.

This can help offset the isolation you may have encountered within your family or civilian community. Surviving fathers communicate and support each other in their own way. This can give you the chance to put your grief into action by reaching out to other surviving fathers.

LESSON LEARNED

Men and women both benefit from understanding the different ways to grieve.

SUMMING IT UP

On top of the traumatic grief of your child's death, as a father you must contend with years of ingrained conditioning and societal stereotypes of men in general and male grief in particular. Additionally, men and women are likely unaware of their inherent preferences for dealing with grief. It's easy to see how surviving fathers may find themselves in a tough spot, especially when remaining in control feels like the right thing to do.

Knowing about the freedom to grieve without judgment goes a long way toward helping you work through grief. And if you're a spouse, girlfriend, or partner, a better understanding of how men grieve will help you, too.

CHAPTER 10

Disenfranchised Grief

I was Trevor's dad. I married his mother, Carlie, when he was two years old. I was the one who taught him how to ride a bike and helped him with his homework. I was the one who waited with Carlie in the emergency room after his car accident. I was the one who Trevor called Dad.

I don't have the right words to describe the night the Army rang our doorbell. I saw them through the peephole; I knew why they were here. It wasn't the news we were dreading—it was worse. Trevor had died from a self-inflicted gunshot wound earlier in the day. He was on his first tour in Afghanistan.

A few weeks later, a letter of condolence came from the president. As Carlie and I read it, we both noticed this letter was addressed only to her. In the following weeks, I came to learn that I wasn't included in the letter because I'm not Trevor's biological father, not his next of kin. Really? I was Trevor's dad.

Nolan (Georgia)

Today's America holds preconceived ideas about military loss. Perhaps due to the public nature of some deaths or how military loss is portrayed in the media and entertainment industry, Americans often make assumptions about how service members die, who makes up the surviving family, and how they should conduct themselves.

All too often, the realities of military loss don't match up with the nation's perceptions of it. When this happens, surviving mothers and fathers may not get the validation they need or the support they deserve.

If you feel that your relationship with your son or daughter is not fully recognized or valued; the impact of your child's death is minimized or overlooked; the cause of death is stigmatizing, embarrassing, or causes anxiety in others; you are left out of funeral or memorial rituals; or your grieving style isn't supported, then your grief may be disenfranchised.

DISENFRANCHISED GRIEF

Noted psychologist and author Kenneth Doka developed the concept of disenfranchised grief. According to Doka, disenfranchised grief results from "a loss that people experience that is not openly acknowledged, socially validated, or publicly observed."

As a Gold Star parent, you may experience disenfranchised grief due to a number of contributing factors. These include:

- Your relationship with your child is minimized or not respected.
- Your loss is not fully acknowledged.
- Your support is affected by the circumstances of the death.
- Your grieving style is not validated.
- You are not included in the rituals of public mourning.

Your Relationship with Your Child Is Minimized or Not Respected

Families come in a variety of shapes and sizes. One-half of today's families are traditional nuclear families, according to the American Academy of Pediatrics (AAP), while the other half may be adoptive, step-, or foster families; have single, never-married, or same-sex parents; or be cross-generational, where grandparents have a major role in child rearing. The bonds formed within these families are sometimes closer than nuclear family ties.

★

PARENT-TO-PARENT

"My ex-wife and I divorced, but I did not divorce my son."

If you are part of a modern family, you may feel as if you've been cast aside because you're not a blood relative or the primary custodial parent. Likewise, the relationship you had with your son or daughter may not be properly recognized or valued by other family members, by the larger community, or within the government hierarchy that operates by the letter of the law. When tragedy strikes, the legal definition of "next of kin" trumps relationships of attachment and commitment. This can occur in a variety of family circumstances:

People who have never lost a child may think it's less devastating for parents to lose an adult son or daughter.

- You're a stepparent who raised your spouse's child as your own.
- You're a custodial foster parent.
- You're a divorced parent without custody or visitation rights.
- Your child was raised by another family member.

Your Loss Is Not Fully Acknowledged

People who have never lost a child may think it's less devastating for parents to lose an adult son or daughter. This is especially true if that child is married with a family or lives a good distance away.

As a surviving parent of an adult child, you may sense that the depth of your loss is not fully understood and/or supported. This may occur when:

- Your child's surviving spouse and/or children legally and emotionally overshadow your loss.
- Your adult child lived on her own and wasn't a physical part of your daily home life.
- Your loss is minimized because you are an adoptive, step-, or foster parent.
- Your former spouse downplays your loss.
- You live in a place where few knew your son.
- You were estranged from your child at the time of death.

Your Support Is Affected by the Circumstances of the Death

Many individuals think service members only die in wartime. When military deaths occur outside of war, some may see these deaths as less deserving of sympathy and support for the survivors, both publicly and privately.

★

PARENT-TO-PARENT

"The way my son died made him no less of a good soldier."

When military deaths occur outside of war, some may see these deaths as less deserving of sympathy and support for the survivors, both publicly and privately.

How your child died has an impact on how you cope with it in the present and what you'll contend with afterward. The cause of death may also affect how well you handle the necessary grief work and where you can find understanding and genuine support. Here are some causes of death that may alter the sympathy and support you receive:

- Your daughter died on active duty, but not in combat.
- The location and circumstances of the death are classified.
- Your son died by suicide.

- The cause of death is embarrassing.
- Your child's death was self-destructive.
- Others died with your daughter because of her actions.
- Your son died by willful misconduct deemed not in the line of duty.
- You son died after he separated from the military.

Your Grieving Style Is Not Validated

Our American society also has unwritten expectations about how people should grieve, what that grief should look like, and how it should be expressed. This is particularly true with military loss where personal grief is likely to cross paths with patriotism and publicity.

When your grief doesn't match up with these expectations, people may judge you as not being affected by the loss of your child and withhold support for you. Here are some circumstances where your grief may be misjudged:

- Your ability to control your emotions is seen as a lack of attachment to your child.
- Your intense grief makes others uncomfortable.
- You grieve through thoughts and actions, rather than emotions.
- You put up a false front for others.
- Your ethnic, cultural, or religious customs are misunderstood.

You're Not Included in the Rituals of Public Mourning

A funeral or memorial service is an outward expression of mourning and a part of grief for all who are present.

A funeral or memorial service is an outward expression of mourning and a part of grief for all who are present. This is especially true for parents, as these rites and services give them the chance to publicly mourn and also the opportunity to receive sympathy and support.

For many moms and dads, having a say in how and where their child is laid to rest is critically important to accepting the reality of the loss. Yet, if you're the Gold Star parent of a married service member, you're not the primary next of kin and may not be the person who is authorized to make funeral and burial decisions.

If your relationship with your son's spouse is tense or contentious—as is sometimes the case between mothers-in-law and daughters-in-law—your burial and funeral wishes for your son may not have been asked for, seriously considered, or acted upon.

As the parent of a married child, you may have felt that your presence at the funeral wasn't properly identified, and your rightful role as a grieving parent wasn't given the acknowledgment or respect it deserved. Here are some situations where you may feel this way:

- You were not included in funeral and burial decisions.
- You were invited to the funeral services but not identified.
- You were unable to attend because of health or age issues.
- You were excluded from the funeral services by a family member.

YOUR REACTIONS TO DISENFRANCHISED GRIEF

If you recognize yourself in any of the above circumstances or others like them, your grief may be disenfranchised. As with everything else in grief, disenfranchisement comes in many ways and in varying degrees.

... disenfranchisement comes in many ways and in varying degrees.

With disenfranchised grief, you may experience significantly intensified reactions. For example, your feelings of sorrow, guilt, and anger may be heightened. Likewise, at this time of emotional wounding, the lack of appropriate sympathy and support can cause you to feel less important as a family member and possibly as a person. This may result in feeling unworthy of normal attention and care, which in turn may cause you to separate yourself from others and further compound your already complicated grief.

HOW YOU CAN HELP YOURSELF

If you believe you've been disenfranchised, the validation you need from your personal community of family and friends may be missing. It may be necessary to look beyond family and friends to find validation of your loss and appropriate support. Here are a few ways to get the support you're looking for:

- Look to others who share your circumstances. They'll understand you without judgment. For instance, seek out the support of other stepparents who have lost a son or daughter or other moms and dads whose child died after separating from the military.
- Create a ritual, ceremony, or action that is significant to you. Rituals and ceremonies don't need to be formal or religious; they can be simple and personal. Flying your flag each day is one such action.
- Try counseling. You'll likely find the validation you need, plus the chance to vent your feelings over the type and amount of recognition and support you did—or did not—receive.

LESSON LEARNED

Disenfranchisement further complicates your grief.

SUMMING IT UP

It's important to recognize your feelings of disenfranchisement as legitimate ones and not disregard them as "too emotional" or "overly sensitive." They are valid feelings.

The recognition of your relationship with your child, the acknowledgment of your profound loss, and the public support of others all contribute to helping you do the work that grief demands.

★

Handling Holidays and Important Days of Meaning

My family doesn't understand me, especially our surviving sons and our daughter. Our kids were really just babies when their brother, Cory, was killed—too young to understand death like an adult. We're almost five years out now, and the oldest one is a teenager, acting like the entire world revolves around him.

I can't believe the fifth anniversary of our Cory's death is coming up later this year. This five-year mark keeps gnawing at me, just like a squirrel gnaws on a tree branch. I mentioned to my husband and the kids that we should do something special on that day this year. Well, you should have heard the reactions I got from the kids. My oldest living son told me that I treat the day Cory was killed like it was Memorial Day. That hurt. And then I thought, What a great idea!

Evelyn (Michigan)

Imagine a calendar year as a highway that starts on January 1 and ends on December 31. Like many a road, this well-traveled highway has a couple of twists and turns, some uneventful stretches, and not enough rest stops. And it has potholes.

Now, imagine your own personal highway through a calendar year. On your highway, holidays and important days are emotional potholes on your private road through loss and grief. Like real potholes, these significant days come in a variety of shapes and sizes. After hitting the first one, you realize you must be on guard for them. Because these days come around each year, it's good to understand why they push so many of your emotional buttons. It's also good to have a plan for managing these important days before they arrive.

HOLIDAYS

A holiday is a special day born out of significance, tradition, or law. It is often distinguished from a regular day by specific actions and customs. A holiday is frequently celebrated or acknowledged by two

A holiday can be emotionally cruel to those who are grieving. or more people coming together, such as a family gathering, a religious service, or a local or national observance.

A holiday can be emotionally cruel to those who are grieving. Just the word *holiday* can make a Gold Star parent cringe. Typically, a holiday is chock-full of tradition. And tradition means memories. For surviving parents, holiday memories are another reminder of the loss of your son or daughter.

TYPES OF HOLIDAYS AND IMPORTANT DAYS

Significant days—those holidays and important days that are meaningful to you—can be grouped into general categories. Each category and day will have personal meaning for you, depending upon who you are, what you believe, and how you've observed or acknowledged these days in the past.

National Holidays Honoring Service Members

America has set aside two days each year to honor its fallen service members and veterans. Memorial Day, observed on the last Monday of May, honors the service-men and -women who have fought and died in America's wars and those who have honorably died while serving in its armed forces. Veterans Day, always observed on November 11, honors America's veterans who are currently serving and those who have proudly served, either living or dead.

Since your child died, Memorial Day and, to a large degree, Veterans Day now have personal importance to you, in addition to their national significance. How could they not? They are national holidays that honor *your* son or daughter. These days tend to be emotionally draining as well as physically exhausting for Gold Star parents. But you already know this from experience, especially if you've attended or taken part in memorial or remembrance ceremonies.

Traditional Holiday Season

The holiday season refers to the end-of-the-year holidays of Thanksgiving, Hanukkah, Christmas, Kwanzaa, and New Year's Day. This season officially begins in mid-November, even though stores begin putting out Christmas displays in mid-August. The holiday season of Thanksgiving through New Year's lasts about six weeks. It just seems longer.

Holidays are usually stressful times; this was true even when your child was still with you.

These holidays are usually family-centered times, celebrated as a season of good cheer and holiday spirit. More often than not, family members make a special effort to connect with loved ones and friends, both near and far. Holidays are usually stressful times; this was true even when your child was still with you. Loss and grief make it worse.

★

PARENT-TO-PARENT

"I'm hibernating through the holidays this year. Wake me up in mid-January."

Holidays don't always go smoothly. As a surviving parent, you may have the tendency to look back on past ones through rose-colored glasses. Not all of those times were wonderful, though. Realistically, no holiday or family is picture-perfect. Each has its own unwritten rules, quirks, and, sometimes, a dysfunctional family member or two. Grief does nothing to make the holidays less stressful and more bearable, nor does it improve family dynamics.

Grief does nothing to make the holidays less stressful and more bearable, nor does it improve family dynamics. You can fake happy and merry for only so long.

You can fake *happy* and *merry* for only so long. It takes a great deal of physical and emotional energy to get through the holidays, with or without the burden of grief. You may have noticed your feelings of grief are heightened during the holiday season and you may feel you've slipped backward. It's normal to feel this way. After the emotional turmoil of the holidays settles down, you'll probably see your grief has settled down as well and you may have even made a little progress by surviving the holidays.

★

PARENT-TO-PARENT

"My son is dead. Don't wish me a 'happy' anything."

Mother's Day and Father's Day

May and June are emotion-laden months for Gold Star parents. Mother's Day is celebrated on the second Sunday of May, with Memorial Day nipping at its heels. Father's Day always falls on the third Sunday of June. These two holidays are focused parent-child days regardless of the age of the parent or the child.

As a surviving mother or father, you can't escape the reality these two days highlight or the pain they bring with them. Mother's Day and Father's Day have the power to magnify your loss because even though they're nationally recognized holidays, they're celebrated in a personal way by parents and their children.

"My son was killed on the Friday before Father's Day weekend," remembered Henry. "Weeks later, my wife found the unopened Father's Day card he sent me, mixed in with a stack of sympathy cards. I opened his card, and it was pretty rough reading. I'm almost six years out now, and I put on a good front for my grandkids every Father's Day, but it's not the same." Then, with awkward hesitation, Henry added, "Please don't tell them I said this."

Religious Holidays

Religious holidays are rooted in the belief system of a faith community. They may include centuries-old traditions and customs and sacred rituals at a church, synagogue, or place of worship. Families often gather to observe a religious holiday with customs that are meaningful to them, passing down the traditions of their faith and family lineage from generation to generation.

There are certain days that have a deeply personal meaning only to you ...

At these times, you may experience not only the loss of your son or daughter, but also the loss of your child's role in preserving the traditions and customs that you hold dear. This may be one of those secondary losses you learned about in Chapter Three.

PERSONAL DAYS OF MEANING

There are certain days that have a deeply personal meaning only to you—once again, because of who you are and the quality of your relationship with your child. These significant days include, but are not limited to: your birthday, your son or daughter's birthday, your child's date of death (sometimes called the "angelversary"), the official military notification date, and the date of your child's military funeral, to name just a few.

These days can be hard. You may feel your reactions are completely misunderstood—and sometimes misjudged—on these personal days of meaning. Few can relate to the private nature and circumstances of your loss.

In a permanent way, the day your child died and, if different, the day you were notified are seared into your memory like acid-etched glass. With vivid clarity you can recall where you were and how you learned of your son or daughter's death. These traumatic memories last a lifetime. "On the day our son was killed, my wife and I usually don't watch the news or read the newspaper," said Benjamin. "Even after all these years, we prefer not to hear that date spoken aloud or see it in print."

> *In a permanent way, the day your child died and, if different, the day you were notified are seared into your memory like acid-etched glass.*

THE DREADED FIRSTS

That first year after your son or daughter died is an endless highway of holiday unknowns: the *first* birthday, the *first* date of death, the *first* set of holidays, and a procession of other firsts of personal meaning.

As the year unfolds, each of these firsts looms large before you, much like a full moon rising over a choppy ocean. Facing these unknowns can create large amounts of anxiety within you, starting a few weeks beforehand and steadily increasing in the days leading up to the holiday or significant date. "With each important date, I turn back time and remember every moment I had with my son in the days beforehand," said Ava.

In addition to your daytime anxiety, there are the sleepless nights. Thoughts such as *How am I going to get through that day?* may endlessly run through your mind. The answer to this question and others like it is hard to find at 3:00 a.m. This is all normal.

MARKERS OF TIME

Men and women of all ages like to measure time. Little kids count the days until they have a birthday and turn another year older. America elects a president to a four-year term of office. Your son or daughter committed to military service for either an enlistment period or an obligated number of years. Generally, people use conventional and accepted measures of time on a regular basis: that four-year term of office, a six-year service obligation, or a ten-year anniversary.

The Merriam-Webster dictionary defines the word *anniversary* as "a date that is remembered or celebrated because a special or notable event occurred on that date in a previous year." Like most people, you probably associate the word *anniversary* with a happy or joyous event: a twenty-fifth wedding anniversary or the fortieth anniversary of the establishment of a favorite restaurant. On occasion, you may hear of a solemn anniversary, such as the anniversary of the September 11 attacks. While you sometimes hear the word associated with death, the phrase *the anniversary of the death* just doesn't sound right. It sounds even worse when it's the anniversary of your child's death.

Markers of time are important in death just as they are in life.

Markers of time are important in death just as they are in life. The anniversary of your child's death is always a hard day in any calendar year. But why are some death anniversaries harder to contend with than others? Certain anniversaries are benchmarks, recognizable and noteworthy measures of time, such as the five-, ten-, or fifteen-year mark since your son or daughter's death. These noteworthy anniversaries seem to possess an unconscious time clock within you—capable of swiftly taking you back to that life-changing day and resurrecting an upsurge of traumatic memories and formidable emotions.

On these benchmark anniversaries, in addition to feeling the loss of your child on a deeper level, you may have the tendency to take stock of life, looking backward to your child's death and reflecting on the time that has passed. You may also evaluate who you are now and where you may want to focus your energy and interests in the future. These noteworthy benchmarks are your personal reality checks on life, death, grief, adjustment, and peace of mind.

HANDLING HOLIDAYS AND IMPORTANT DAYS OF MEANING

As with most things in life, there is no one-size-fits-all solution for dealing with holidays and days of meaning. But, with some planning

Have a plan for the day. Be extra good to yourself.
and a little determination, you can find ways to make significant dates better for you and those around you. Start with this premise: Have a plan for the day. Be extra good to yourself. And remember:

- Your emotions are raw. Protect them as you would an open wound.
- Grief makes you hypersensitive. Keep this thought nearby.
- Your approach to holidays and days of meaning will evolve over the years.

Handling holidays and important days of meaning is never easy. And some days can be harder than others. As you move forward, you'll learn what works for you—and what doesn't. In the process of learning, though, you can be proactive before these days occur.

Here are seven ideas to make holidays and important days more tolerable:

1. **Simplify.** Especially for holidays, make a list of all the things you have to do. Before starting to work the list, sort it into manageable categories:

- Must-do things.
- Nice-to-do things.
- Why am I doing these things?

By breaking down your list, you've prioritized what must be done and, hopefully, shortened your to-do list by eliminating those nonessential items. This can save you time and energy, which are often in short supply.

2. **Practice.** Practicing for a holiday or an event may sound silly. In all likelihood, you can't practice physically, but you can mentally rehearse the day or event as you believe it will unfold. For example, if you're going to a memorial ceremony, visualize a sea of military uniforms, the presentation of colors, and the singing of the national anthem. By doing a mental rehearsal, you're anticipating what will happen, increasing the likelihood you'll be better prepared to handle the military presence and ceremonial traditions. Mental rehearsals are easy, and you can do them on your own. You may be surprised at their value.

3. **Choose to celebrate a holiday on another date.** Let's say Christmas is a particularly tough holiday for you. While you can't make the decorations, advertisements, and merriment disappear, you can celebrate Christmas at another time of the year with your family. To some this may sound crazy—or not. But you may find a pleasant sense of control by celebrating Christmas in August—on your own terms—perhaps with an outdoor tree and a backyard party. Or how about Mother's Day in January? The possibilities are endless.

4. **Be extra good to yourself.** Stock up on energy; make it a point to eat right and get enough sleep. Pamper yourself before

and after a meaningful day, if that's what works for you. Do something you enjoy that will recharge your physical and emotional batteries. Put time into a hobby or an activity that gives you pleasure and a sense of accomplishment.

5. **Remember your child in an appropriate, meaningful, and healthy way.** It's important to remember your child; it's also important to incorporate his or her memory while being rooted in the present. Especially on holidays, carefully choose how to integrate your child's memory into the day without overwhelming yourself. Try not to make those around you overly uncomfortable.

6. **Limit your time with people who ooze negativity.** Your physical and emotional energy is a precious resource, especially now. Guard this resource by minimizing the time you spend with energy-zapping, negative people. For example, those toxic relatives you *must* see at the holidays? If you can't avoid seeing them, come up with a plan to minimize the amount of time you must spend with them. Give yourself frequent breaks, even if it means stepping outside for a head-clearing gulp of fresh air.

7. **Set time limits.** Keep in mind that you don't need to stay to the end of an event, party, or family gathering. It's okay to leave early. And you don't need to explain to everyone why you're leaving. Have a polite but firm exit strategy.

Hopefully these ideas will get you thinking about how to approach holidays and days of meaning in different ways. Think outside that proverbial box for other ideas. It may be hard to believe in your early years of grief, but how you handle holidays will evolve from year to year, and eventually you may find comfort and enjoyment in some of those holidays.

LESSON LEARNED

Days of meaning are tough, but with some outside-the-box planning you can have some influence over them.

SUMMING IT UP

As Gold Star parents, you face extra holidays and days of meaning each calendar year. These days can add more stress and another layer of complexity to your already complicated grief.

While it isn't easy, the best way to get through holidays and days of meaning is to have a plan for those times. And take extra good physical and emotional care of yourself before, during, and after them.

★

Part Five

Building
Personal
Resilience

CHAPTER 12

Moving Forward

Just a few weeks after my son Patrick was killed, Jenn, a surviving mother who lived in my state, reached out to me. She had also lost her son in the military and, like myself, was divorced. We instantly connected and became kindred spirits on this unplanned journey through living hell. She was a lifeline for me because no one I knew ever lost a child, much less one in the military. Jenn "got it," sometimes even without words being said.

I'm shy around strangers and didn't want to leave my townhouse too often. After I wallowed in grief for a few months, Jenn asked me if Pat would want me to fritter my life away. That day, I decided that death and grief were not going to get the best of me.

Working on my grief wasn't easy. Through Jenn I learned about TAPS, the Army's Survivor Outreach Services (SOS), and the local chapter of Gold Star Mothers. Each one has helped me tremendously.

I can honestly say that my good days outnumber the bad ones now, and I'm grateful for it.

Denise (Florida)

L ife never has the same feel after the death of a child. Nor should it. As a parent, you're left to cope with the way your life should be and the way it is. It's a lifelong adjustment.

Part of that adjustment means facing your child's death and working through the grief as best as you can. A great loss such as this produces great pain and grief. But try not to let grief hold you hostage for the rest of your earthly days.

Healing doesn't mean leaving your child in the past; it simply means gaining the strength to make your way in life without your son or daughter.

Another part of your adjustment is healing your body, mind, and spirit, for healing is a part of grief. Healing doesn't mean leaving your child in the past; it simply means gaining the strength to make your way in life without your son or daughter. As you make your way, you'll find your grief changes, too. While this usually happens more slowly than you'd like, there will come a time when grief loses its hold on you, and you may even feel a twinge of guilt when it happens. You're not alone.

"When I realized I didn't cry one day," said Aracelli, "I felt that I was leaving my son behind." However, Aracelli soon came to realize she wasn't leaving him behind; she was bringing her son along in memory as she gained strength in body, mind, and spirit.

MOVING ON

Moving on is another clichéd term in the language of grief. Many survivors take exception to it, and rightfully so. To the griever, moving on implies breaking the physical and emotional ties to people, places, and things. It conveys letting go and putting the past behind. And moving on alludes to trying to forget. Gold Star parents do none of these things.

MOVING FORWARD

Moving forward will have different meanings at different times in your grief. Early on, when survival was your priority, movement may have meant simply getting out of bed and facing the day. "I hated when I was told to 'take it one day at a time,'" said Cindy, "especially when I was trying to figure out how to make it through the next hour." Cindy did make it through the hour and the many more that followed.

In grief's most painful times, moving forward may seem impossible. Yet, even in the midst of pain, you inch forward. Just as your child learned to walk with baby steps, you learn to take baby steps through grief until you're ready to stand on your own.

Just as your child learned to walk with baby steps, you learn to take baby steps through grief until you're ready to stand on your own.

You may not be aware that you're moving forward in grief until you look back on how far you've come. It's a good idea to look back from time to time and take note of your progress. Seeing this progress is encouraging.

THE FIRST YEAR

The first year is numbing. A child's death is always traumatic, and as a Gold Star parent, you're faced with additional circumstances unique to military loss.

For instance, the military's casualty notification process has been described by many as traumatic, given its formality and the news that's delivered. Likewise, feelings of denial may be exacerbated if your child was deployed or the remains weren't viewable or recoverable. And if your child died on a classified mission, you may not be able to talk about it openly, denying you a real need in the grief process. These are just a few examples of circumstances that surviving parents may cope with in the first year.

The support you received immediately after your child's death probably dwindled considerably after the funeral. Family, friends, and military personnel may have unconsciously sought a breather from the intensity of your son or daughter's death and backed away, needing to return to the routine of their own lives and recharge their own emotional batteries.

If you're the primary next of kin, you likely had continued support from your casualty officer, but the casualty process generally wraps up within thirty to forty days, and then the casualty officer returns to his or her primary duties. By the three-month mark, the world usually stops grieving with you, even though you've barely scratched the surface of your grief.

THE SECOND YEAR

Psychologists and survivors alike have often called the second year "the lonely year." In many ways, the second year is harder to cope with than the first one. The shock and numbness of the first year have worn off and the harshness of reality confronts you again and again. Your awareness that your child is dead takes on new levels.

Psychologists and survivors alike have often called the second year "the lonely year."

America's tolerance for grief is limited. By the second year, most of the world unrealistically expects you to be "doing fine"—whatever that means. "A friend said she didn't mention my daughter Sarah on her second angelversary because she didn't want to upset me," recalled Anne. "It's not like I forgot. What she didn't realize was how much she upset me by *not* mentioning her."

THE FOLLOWING YEARS

Earlier in this book, you learned that your grief is like a perfect storm, built upon the intersection of those three powerful forces: your child's death, the likelihood that it was sudden and unexpected, and the multifaceted elements that military service brings to death. Complex grief such as this usually requires a considerable amount of work, time, and patience.

It's important to remember that working through your grief involves more than just feeling the pain of your child's death. A part of your grief work is to continually adapt to a world without your son or daughter. Another aspect of your grief work is to make meaning of your child's life and, possibly, your own as well. In doing so, you may be surprised to learn who you are now, and how you've grown in inner strength and resilience.

The following years are also a time to repair and renew relationships that have been neglected by grief ...

The following years are also a time to repair and renew relationships that have been neglected by grief, such as those with your family, friends, and the God you believe in. Your child's death had a ripple effect well beyond you, and many others have felt its impact.

With perseverance and grief work, you're learning to live with a more manageable level of grief, one that doesn't constantly interfere with picking up the pieces of your life and reshaping it in light of the loss you've suffered. It's also a time to reinvest in life in ways that are less painful. You'll probably find the need to reinvest in life again and again. As with everything else in grief, start slowly and adjust often.

There's wisdom in the phrase, "grief doesn't have a timetable." And it would be unwise to curtail—or extend—your grief to meet another person's expectations.

For Gold Star parents, moving forward never ends. It's a lifelong adjustment to live in a world without your son or daughter. Life does go on; it just goes on very differently.

Moving forward is both personal and shared. Like grief, it has a ripple effect in your life, affecting your family and friends and your relationships with them. Moving forward happens in large and small ways. Sometimes you move forward without being aware of it through a wide range of actions. Surviving parents have moved forward in grief using some of these ways:

- Getting out of bed and not dreading the day.
- Feeling sad one moment and happy the next.
- Balancing a fragile present with the pull of the past.
- Thinking more of your child's life than the circumstances of the death.
- No longer bringing up your child's death in every conversation.
- Seeing that levels of grief and peace of mind can coexist.
- Finding comfort in memories of your son or daughter.
- Enjoying yourself and not feeling (too) guilty.
- Taking a time-out from grief.
- Reinvesting in life without guilt.
- Building personal resiliency and strength.

BUMPS IN THE ROAD

Moving forward in grief doesn't always go smoothly. You've learned from experience that grief doesn't respect progress. The catchphrase

… moving two steps forward and one step backward is still progress.

"two steps forward, one step backward" probably sums up your grief quite well. While you may be discouraged when your progress forward is offset by a step backward, keep in mind that moving two steps forward and one step backward is still progress. You're moving in the right direction. And slow progress is better than no progress at all.

Here are some bumps in the road other Gold Star parents have experienced. You may have additional ones.

Memorial Overload

Another unique element of military loss is the potential of multiple memorial services, both immediately after the death and well into the future. It's possible there may have been multiple memorial or dedication services in different locations for your child. In addition to the funeral, there may have been other remembrances, such as at your child's last duty station, at schools he or she attended, in your hometown, or at your church, synagogue, or place of worship.

... you can reach a point where your ability to cope with additional emotions has reached its limits.

As the surviving parent, you may have been invited to attend or asked to participate in many of these remembrances. Undoubtedly, you appreciated the recognition for your child. If you experienced multiple memorials, you may have found these many services both personally rewarding and emotionally draining. The emotions generated by these events have a tendency to accumulate, and it can become too painful to attend them. This is a normal reaction, a grief overload. Yet, as a parent, you likely felt guilty about declining an invitation. Try not to feel guilty—you can reach a point where your ability to cope with additional emotions has reached its limits. This is usually a good time to step back and recharge your batteries.

Also keep in mind that there may come a day when you opt not to attend an emotionally stirring event related to the military or a national holiday. The emotional upheaval may be too hard to handle, especially if there are other stressors in your life. "This year, I decided not to attend the local Memorial Day ceremony," said Frank. "It isn't because I don't care anymore, it's just that I go to the ceremony every year and it stirs everything up. When it's over, everyone else goes on to his or her backyard cookout, and I go home alone. I just don't want to stir things up this year. I'll remember my son in my own way on Memorial Day."

Changing Circumstances

It's important for you to know the circumstances that led up to your child's death, his or her last actions, and what unfolded afterward. This is normal in grief, particularly if your child's death was sudden and unexpected. It's not uncommon to be obsessed with every detail, especially early on, when you struggled with the reality that your child was indeed dead. As reality began to sink in, this obsession probably lessened its hold on you, but your desire to know those last moments may never completely go away.

Bursts of grief are sudden and unpredictable occurrences of powerful grief reactions. With some military deaths, it takes time to piece together the details or conduct investigations. It's possible you may learn additional information about your child's death weeks, months, or years later. This new information may conflict with what you've come to understand about the death, possibly introducing a new perspective on how and why your child died. This can be upsetting. Whether it's been five months or five years, learning new details about the final moments of your child's life can bring on intense grief reactions. And you may feel as though you're re-grieving your child's death with this new information.

Bursts of Grief

Bursts of grief are sudden and unpredictable occurrences of powerful grief reactions. Also called *grief attacks* or *grief spasms*, they've been described as pangs or waves of grief. By whatever name you call them, these bursts of grief can be overpowering. When they happen, you may feel like you've been transported back to a particularly intense time in your grief. "I was born and raised in California," explained Maria, "and I've come to think of grief attacks as my own personal aftershocks. They're not as powerful as the earthshaking news of my daughter's death, but they do knock me for a loop."

Grief attacks can come out of nowhere and occur for no reason. One moment you're having a good day and the next moment you may be awash with grief. Grief attacks can also be brought on by triggers. In the framework of grief, triggers come from many different sources. They may be caused by:

- Bad news
- Doses of reality
- Secondary losses
- Insensitive remarks
- Benchmarks of time
- Important days of meaning

Grief attacks are common. As you move forward, you'll likely notice that they occur less frequently, and it's easier to recover from them.

Secondary Losses

Earlier in this book, you read about secondary losses. These additional losses stem directly from your child's death. Almost always unanticipated, secondary losses can hit a nerve, and those that hurt the most are probably the most important to you.

The grief over secondary losses can be powerful and long lasting. Because of them, you may feel that the ramifications of your child's death never end.

"When my only child was killed, my chance to become a grandfather was lost," said Andy. "I never realized what that meant until my friends become grandfathers. Then it hit me pretty hard."

The grief over secondary losses can be powerful and long lasting. Because of them, you may feel that the ramifications of your child's death never end.

Dumb Things People Say

Other setbacks may be triggered by what comes out of the mouths of others. As a grieving parent, you need support and validation, which can often be found in organizations, events, and people. But one way you won't find it is through the dumb things some people say, no matter how well intentioned.

It appears to be a universal phenomenon for people to say dumb things to those who are grieving. And it defies explanation as to why they do so. "I had a woman tell me she was happy that I had a 'spare' child," said Glenda. "I was so taken aback that I was speechless, which was probably a good thing."

Death makes many people uncomfortable and—as you know all too well—the death of a child makes them even more so. In the absence of knowing what to say, some people blurt out things that are nothing more than clichés. These comments provide little comfort, and some may come across as disrespectful and hurtful.

It appears to be a universal phenomenon for people to say dumb things to those who are grieving.

Most people who say dumb things aren't out to hurt you. While you may wonder why they've said it, in some obscure way they may believe they're helping you feel better. Sometimes people will try to connect with you through a loss of their own. But the phrase "I know exactly how you feel" usually falls flat. Others may look to ease your pain by saying, "Things happen for a reason," or try to give you hope with "Time heals all wounds."

However well-intentioned people may be, comments such as these usually miss the mark and sound like the tired, old clichés that they are.

CLOSURE

Closure is a versatile word. It has multiple meanings in different circumstances. In the business world, it can convey agreement or completion, such as "The editor sought closure on the news story before the paper went to press." In math classes, closure is a mathematical property. And in cost-conscious economies, it may mean the act of closing or being permanently closed, such as a grocery store, factory, or military installation closure.

In the language of grief, closure doesn't have a place. If you're like most Gold Star parents, you shy away from using the word. Talking about closure doesn't feel right.

In the language of grief, closure doesn't have a place.

Closure is a term frequently heard in the media, and it's often used in elusive ways, such as "seeking closure" or "finding closure." Sometimes it's understood to mean an all-or-nothing occurrence. Either you have closure—or you don't. Its use seems to imply the end of emotional connectedness.

Perhaps there's space between the extremes of all and nothing for a broader understanding of closure. While you probably never thought of closure as a matter of degree, it's conceivable to find some peace of mind in life's tragedies, even your child's death.

But whatever degree of peace of mind you achieve, it should be called something other than closure.

WHEN MOVING FORWARD ISN'T "MOVING FORWARD"

You know from experience that grief is a hard and often problematic journey. And it's one you make without the aid of a GPS device mapping out your every turn and adjusting for the times you wander off course. You also know that some GPS routes are longer than others; eventually, though, each route gets to the destination. As a surviving mom or dad, the sought-after "destination" on your grief journey is a personal place where grief, memories, and a little peace of mind can coexist. And just as with GPS routes, there's more than one way to get there, as you know from your own grief experiences and reading this book.

When your intense grief lessens, you'll find relief from the weight of it. You'll soon discover you're more capable of handling the ups and downs of everyday living. And you'll likely find you're more invested in yourself, your family, and life in general. There's comfort in feeling a little like your old self again.

Seeking out help is not a sign of failure; it is an act of determination. But what happens when grief doesn't lessen its hold on you? You may have reached a point where you're "stuck" in grief and the healing of your body, mind, and spirit isn't moving forward. If you're feeling stuck—or someone points it out—then it's time to do something about it. The best way to get back on track is to seek a little assistance.

You may balk at the thought of getting help with grief, so think about it this way: your child's death is the toughest loss you will ever confront, and it may take a little specialized guidance to make your way through its roughest parts. You actually turn to specialists all the time without giving it a second thought. For example, if you're plagued with back pain that you can't fix with a heating pad or over-the-counter pain relievers, you'll probably see a chiropractor or an orthopedic doctor to get some relief. This same logic applies for grief.

If you feel that you're stuck in grief—or you're unwilling to let go of your intense grief for your child—then the time has likely come to look for a little help. Seeking out help is not a sign of failure; it's an act of determination. Being stuck in grief need not be a permanent state.

LESSON LEARNED

Two steps forward and one step backward is still progress.

SUMMING IT UP

Moving forward is as much a process as it is a direction. Early on, it may look like wobbly baby steps, while later in your grief journey, moving forward can be found in the choices you make and the risks you take. As with everything else in grief, moving forward takes some work and lots of determination. Perseverance is found in progress— and you're worth it.

★

CHAPTER 13

Building Personal Resiliance

I know I've changed since Eric's death, but I never realized how different I looked until I ran into Lyn, the mother of Eric's best friend from high school. It was an awkward moment when she didn't recognize me, but Lyn recovered nicely. The look in her eyes was another story.

Later that day, I took a hard look in the mirror and asked, "Who is this person?" With a little wry humor, I thought I now looked as bad on the outside as I felt on the inside. I had stopped caring about myself and it showed.

I can't say I jumped onto the health-and-fitness bandwagon, but I did start making a few changes. I got outside more and discovered I liked taking walks. Before I knew it, my walks got longer and I was moving a little faster. I also cut back on fast food. I figured there was no sense in wasting a good walk on food that was bad for me.

As a result of getting outside and eating a little smarter, I began to feel better. And I dropped down a pants size, too.

Chris (Pennsylvania)

Grief is an energy hog. It gobbles up your daily energy whenever it can. Think of your energy as gas in your personal tank. You use a gallon or two every day, just to keep your body running. The rest you use on the essentials of daily life, as well as the people, places, and things that need your time and attention. You can only hold so much gas in your personal tank on any given day, and when it's used up—it's used up. You're out of energy, regardless of the time of day or the things you still need to do.

Energy helps you get through the day, but resilience moves you forward in the long haul.

Most people would like to have more energy. While you can't buy it, you can set in motion the means to give yourself additional energy every day, and the skills to use it more effectively.

Energy helps you get through the day, but resilience moves you forward in the long haul. What is resilience? While it has different meanings in science, health, and psychology, a solid definition is found on www.merriam-webster.com, where resilience is defined as "the ability to recover from or adjust easily to misfortune or change."

On a personal level, resilience can mean having the doggedness to persevere, the backbone to get up again when life has knocked you down, or the grit and guts to not let grief win.

You already have resilience, but in times of hardship and adversity, you can always use a little more. Here are fourteen proven ways to maintain or increase your personal resilience:

1. **Improve your eating habits.** Your old eating habits probably flew out the window when your child died, and this may have happened without your awareness. Perhaps you were the parent who lost interest in food and sometimes forgot to eat. Or you were the one who ate everything in sight, even when you weren't hungry. People eat—or don't eat—for many different reasons. What you eat can affect your health, mood, and general outlook on life.

   There's something to be said for comfort food, but a regular diet of it isn't a good idea. While fat, sugar, and salt may taste good, they don't supply the lasting energy you need to grieve for your child, and to take care of basic needs in your life.

Think back to the days when your child was a youngster. There's little doubt you told him or her to eat all the fruits and vegetables, finish the milk, and stay away from junk food.

While fat, sugar, and salt may taste good, they don't supply the lasting energy you need …

This good advice applies to Gold Star mothers and fathers, too.

One way to look at what you eat is to think of your body as an engine, much like the engine in your car. When you put the right type of fuel in the tank, it runs like a charm. The same goes for what you eat. With the right kinds of "fuel" in your tank, you'll run better, too. And you'll have more energy to boot. The food you eat is the fuel you put into your personal engine:

Food = Fuel = Energy

A good way to learn more about healthy eating is to check out the President's Council on Fitness, Sports & Nutrition, www.fitness.gov, and click on the "Eat Healthy" tab.

2. **Get moving.** You've heard many times about the health benefits of exercise, but who wants to think about exercising when you don't feel like doing much of anything? This may be precisely the time not only to think about exercising, but also to simply get up and get moving.

Physical activity is good for you. It also comes in many forms—a walk outside, a physically active hobby, individual or group exercise, or manual labor—and the benefits are many. Exercise in any form can be a stress buster, as well as a way to work at your grief. Remember, grief is more than simply emotional responses, and some people work through their grief with physical activity.

It helps to find a physical activity you like doing—that way, you'll do more of it.

You may also find being active helps to raise your mood, have more energy, get rid of your anger, and improve your sleep, to name a few additional benefits.

It helps to find a physical activity you like doing—that way, you'll do more of it. And it's good to find an exercise buddy for motivation and company. Be smart and check with a healthcare professional before starting to exercise, especially now, as grief can change how your body functions.

The American Heart Association offers great tips on how to get moving. Go to www.heart.org and type "get moving" into the search box.

3. **Keep up a routine.** People are creatures of habit. And a string of habits done regularly is often called a routine. You have many routines in an average day, and most of them require little thought or consideration on your part. That's the beauty in daily routines—you don't have to make decisions.

... you'll benefit from establishing a little order and structure to your days ...

You just do what you've always done, whether it's your morning routine to start the day or the one that gets you to and from work. There's an unconscious predictability in your routines, and that's a good feeling.

Your child's death probably fractured your daily routines in the immediate days and weeks afterward, even if your child didn't live with you. The disruption of your daily routines was a loss for you, though you didn't realize it at the time. In times of grief and loss, you'll benefit from establishing a little order and structure to your days, even if it's temporary. This structure will help provide a sense of security and comfort. And it can help reduce anxiety and stress.

As you move forward in grief, it's helpful to rebuild your daily routines and potentially add new ones. Try to include self-care in your new routines, such as getting more physical activity and other positive actions that help to strengthen your body, mind, and spirit.

4. **Get enough sleep.** A good night's sleep is elusive for many surviving mothers and fathers, as trouble sleeping is a common grief reaction. Like many parents, you may have difficulty getting to sleep, staying asleep, or sleeping restfully. And all too often, you wake up tired.

A lack of sleep can also play into your other grief reactions, such as memory lapses, confused thinking, or susceptibility to illnesses. And lack of sleep can make you irritable.

The National Academy of Sciences estimates drowsy drivers cause nearly 20 percent of car accidents.

There are many benefits of regular, restful sleep, and a surprising one is that a good night's sleep can help make you safer—around your house, at your job, and behind the wheel. The National Academy of Sciences estimates drowsy drivers cause nearly 20 percent of car accidents.

When sleep doesn't come easily, there are tips and tricks to help you get the kind of night's sleep you yearn for. Go to www.health.com and type "20 things you shouldn't do before bed." You may be pleasantly surprised at what can help you get a good night's sleep.

5. **Play with your pets.** More than three out of five households have at least one pet, according to the National Pet Products

Association, and the majority of these households see their pets as members of their families.

If you're a pet person, you already know the virtues of having furry companions. Pets provide companionship, love, and a healthy dose of adoring attention, which can help counter those feelings of loneliness and isolation. Pets can make you laugh, which is always a good feeling, and playing with your pet helps to reduce stress. Petting a dog or cat may make you feel calmer, and your pet will like it, too.

Pets can also help you work through grief. They never tire of hearing you talk about your son or daughter, even when you tell the same stories time and again.

Pets can also help you work through grief. They never tire of hearing you talk about your son or daughter, even when you tell the same stories time and again. And a pet often gives you a good reason to get out of bed in the morning. Walking a dog gets you outdoors and moving.

If you've ever had pets, you know they're more than just a pet. Many people have strong bonds with their furry companions, and those bonds work both ways.

6. **Give time to a hobby.** A hobby is "an activity that you do for pleasure when you are not working," according to the Cambridge English Dictionary. Hobbies are activities that individuals want to do, not something they have to do. If you already have a hobby, you know it's something you look forward to working on. No doubt you also find it rewarding and get personal satisfaction from it.

If you've lost interest in your hobby after your child died, this may be a good time to get back into it. A hobby usually requires you to focus on the task at hand, taking you away from grief for a while. It gives you legitimate "permission" to put your energy, time, and attention into something other than grief. And like many other actions on this list, a hobby can help you deal with stress and improve your self-esteem.

If you don't have a hobby, perhaps you want to consider one. Hobbies come in all shapes and sizes, and you may be interested in more than one activity. Try to look beyond the scope of the military and families of the fallen for hobbies and activities that appeal to you. Find out more about the benefits of hobbies at www.psychologytoday.com by typing "six reasons to get a hobby" in the search bar.

> *It gives you legitimate "permission" to put your energy, time, and attention into something other than grief.*

7. **Tap into your religious beliefs and faith community.** In recent Gallup polls, nine out of ten Americans said they believe in God. With this solid statistic, there's a good chance you're part of this God-believing majority of American citizens.

In Chapter Seven, you learned about the spiritual component of grief and the inevitable search for answers to life's toughest questions. You're not alone in this search; people of all faiths have struggled with unanswerable "whys" since time began.

If you're not an active part of a religious community, you may want to look at faith communities, not only as part of your search for meaning, but also as a source of comfort and strength.

It really doesn't matter how much or how little faith you have right now—the community will undoubtedly be welcoming. As a part of a religious community, you may find new personal insights within the services, rituals, traditions, and beliefs of that particular religious faith. Don't be afraid to ask questions of the religious leaders or other men and women of faith whom you meet along the way.

8. **Look for ways to relax.** Time to relax each day is often hard to come by. Many surviving parents lead busy lives, and with the weight of grief slowing them down, they're often exhausted by nightfall. Relaxing may simply mean falling into bed.

If you're one of these parents, you probably wish you had time to relax, but that's often not the case. Your challenge is to find ways to relax that can be measured in minutes, rather than hours, days, or weeks. As you build resilience and move forward, a priority is to make time for yourself and find ways to relax each day. Now is a good time to think about what "being relaxed" feels like and what you normally do to get there. For some old-and-new suggestions on how to relax, search the internet for "ways to relax." You'll find ideas that best suit your personality and lifestyle.

9. **Try to laugh every day.** "Laughter is the best medicine" is an old adage that some say has roots tracing back to the Old Testament of the Bible; it's also a phrase recognized by

Laughter is good for you…. it connects you with life again.

millions of *Reader's Digest* fans as a favorite monthly feature on everyday humor. Whatever its origins, "laughter is the best medicine" is good advice.

Laughter is good for you. It gives you a break from grief, even for just a few seconds—it's hard to laugh and be sad at the same time. Laughter also helps you to relax, as a good laugh goes a long way in relieving tension and stress. You feel good when you laugh—it connects you with life again.

Laughter has health benefits, too. In addition to lightening your mood, laughter can aid in boosting your immunity, decreasing pain, and protecting your heart. Learn more about the benefits of laughter at www.helpguide.org. Search for "laughter is the best medicine."

10. **Maintain your personal relationships.** The first relationship to maintain is with yourself. It isn't hard to lose personal awareness of who you are; grief often robs you of it. And grief can turn you into a stranger—even to yourself. A little "attention to me" time can go a long way toward protecting your body, mind, and spirit.

Grief has a way of stifling personal relationships with family and friends. Maintaining relationships after a child's death can be tough; parental grief is new territory for everyone. Its rippling effects reach far and wide, and family and friends may stay away because of their own uneasiness. All too often, you don't know why they keep their distance.

Unfortunately, you can't control how others behave. But you can try to stay connected to the people who have remained in your immediate circle of family and friends.

11. **Respect your boundaries.** A boundary is an imaginary line where comfort ends and anxiety begins. Everyone has boundaries, but little thought is given to them on any given day.

A boundary is an imaginary line where comfort ends and anxiety begins.

Your old boundaries guarded and guided how you interacted with others and how they interacted with you. Your child's death changed those personal boundaries, a fact you probably learned by trial and error.

A part of moving forward is to become aware of your new vulnerabilities, recognize your hot buttons, and learn to set limits on the people, places, and things that you find

emotionally wounding. This collective awareness will help
shape your new personal boundaries.

Establishing new boundaries gives you the freedom to say "no" without guilt and "yes" by choice.

Establishing new boundaries gives you the
freedom to say "no" without guilt and "yes"
by choice. Please keep in mind that there's a
difference between healthy boundaries and
shutting out the world, which may lead to
isolation and loneliness.

12. **Seek and give support.** Military grief is often isolating, especially
    in communities where little is known about military service.
    Because you've lost both a child and a service member, you
    experience a grief that few understand.

    Given the uniqueness of military grief, there are benefits
    to be gained by connecting with other Gold Star parents.
    With them, you can find an unspoken understanding of
    military loss and, perhaps, the chance to "let your guard
    down." You know that military grief can be complex, and
    it's often easier to be with others who share this grief, rather
    than trying to handle it on your own.

    There's no statute of limitations on reaching out for
    support, so don't be afraid that the time isn't right. Chances
    are there is another mother or father who is wrestling with
    the same issues you are—right now.

    Likewise, you may find it rewarding to help other parents
    who now walk in your shoes. It's an opportunity to use your
    grief for a greater good.

    TAPS has a robust peer-mentoring program. Here
    you will find support in your grief process and also the
    opportunity to put your personal lessons learned to work by
    helping other parents. Check out TAPS at www.taps.org.

13. Get help if stress, anxiety, or depression interferes with your daily life.
You've probably encountered stress reactions or feelings of
anxiety, sadness, or depression as part of your grief journey.
They are common symptoms of grief, and—as you're well
aware—are experienced in fluctuating levels of intensity and
duration. Usually these feelings and reactions dissipate as you
work through the hardest parts of your grief. But what if they
don't lessen in intensity?

It may be hard to differentiate when these reactions
and feelings cross the line and become something more
than grief. It's a good idea to err on the side of caution, so
if you've having trouble contending with stress, anxiety, or
depression on a daily basis, then it's time to look for a little
assistance with addressing them.

You can learn more about the symptoms of stress, anxiety,
and depression at www.helpguide.org. Look at Chapter 8 for
ways to find the right type of help. You can also go to www.
psychologytoday.com and find psychologists, psychiatrists,
and support groups in your zip code.

14. Avoid drinking excessive alcohol. Mixing alcohol with grief may
be tempting, but it's generally not a good idea. Especially
now, it's wise to be mindful of how much alcohol you drink
and how often you do it.

Alcohol is a depressant to your central nervous system,
and its regular use can exacerbate many of your grief
reactions. It can:

- Affect your mood.
- Increase your feelings of depression and anxiety.
- Impair your memory.
- Wreak havoc with your ability to concentrate.

- Slow down your reaction time.
- Alter your motor coordination.

There's a common, but incorrect, belief that alcohol can help you fall asleep and stay asleep, a sought-after state for many parents. While having a drink or two before bedtime may help you fall asleep faster, alcohol is disruptive to staying asleep. Simply said, alcohol is not the means to a good night's sleep.

... alcohol is not the means to a good night's sleep.

Alcohol is a drug, and its heavy use can lead to health problems. Learn more about it at www.webmd.com by typing "12 health risks of chronic heavy drinking" into the search box.

LESSON LEARNED

Building personal resilience strengthens your body, mind, and spirit.

SUMMING IT UP

Building personal resilience is a process. It's a combination of actions you can embrace and enjoy, and their combined effect is greater than the sum of its parts. Resilience has a wonderful way of building upon itself; it has synergy.

There's both comfort and strength in knowing you have personal resilience.

Part Six

What You Need to Know as a Relative, Friend, or Professional Service Provider

CHAPTER 14

★

What You Need to Know

I never expected my son to die while serving in the military. Why would I? When your kid joins up, you have to believe in something greater than yourself. You know you raised a good son, you hope and pray for his safety, and you trust the government will provide your child with the best leadership, training, and equipment.

The last time I saw Jeff there was a confidence in him I had never seen before. My Jeffery seemed so mature now, so "grown up." My heart swelled with pride.

How could I ever be prepared for that knock on the door and the bad news that followed? Why would I even think about something awful happening to my son?

Anita (Illinois)

If you are a relative of a Gold Star parent who lives near or afar, a friend looking for ways to be supportive, or a professional assistance provider operating in unknown territory when it comes to military loss, then this chapter and those to follow are for you. The material you'll find lays out what you need to know about military loss and presents reliable guidance on providing support, not only to Gold Star parents, but also to other family members who have lost a loved one in the line of duty. In this process of learning about military loss and grief, you'll also increase your confidence and skills in this important, sensitive area.

It will be difficult to read these chapters. What you read here may bring up memories of your own past losses. Don't be alarmed. It's a common occurrence.

It will be difficult to read these chapters.... For most people, just thinking about death is uncomfortable, and many instinctively shy away from the topic.

For most people, just thinking about death is uncomfortable, and many instinctively shy away from the topic. If this describes you, know you're in good company. In these helping chapters, you'll find what you need to know, written in language that's easy to take in and put to good use.

Like most of life's burdens, grief doesn't come with an instruction manual. While you may have personally experienced your share of losses, you probably haven't come across the complex grief that usually goes hand in hand with a military death. For Gold Star parents, it's a dual loss, their life-changing personal loss entwined with a lasting national loss. For many people, military and civilian alike, the long-term implications of this dual loss are hard to imagine or understand.

In America today, less than 1 percent of the population has served in the military. Personally knowing an active duty service member and his or her family is an exception, rather than the norm. As a result, many Americans have little knowledge of the military or how it operates. It's safe to say a good deal of what is known about the military comes from the news and social media or the entertainment industry. And these outlets don't always present a realistic picture of military life.

With so few connected to the military, it's common to not know much about the military's individual service branches or how each one fits into the larger military framework. Being comfortably aware of this framework is invaluable, for it helps to connect you with a Gold Star parent's frame of reference, and it helps them feel more at ease with you. While most Gold Star parents have a good understanding of their child's service branch, some aren't as knowledgeable of the other branches.

UNITED STATES MILITARY OVERVIEW

The military, also referred to as the armed forces, is made up of five service branches: the Army, Navy, Air Force, Marine Corps, and Coast Guard. Each branch has a specific mission that's vital to the overall protection and defense of the nation. All the service branches are composed of active-duty and reserve personnel. For example, in the Army there are active-duty (also called regular) soldiers, and reserve soldiers called the Army Reserve. The other service branches follow this structure.

The military, also referred to as the armed forces, is made up of five service branches ...

In addition to the Army, Navy, Air Force, Marine Corps, and Coast Guard, each state has its own National Guard force, usually identified with the state's name—the New Jersey National Guard, for example. These forces can be called up by the state's governor for state emergencies, such as disaster response or other crisis situations. The National Guard can also be activated at a federal level to meet national needs, such as the recent wars in Iraq and Afghanistan where Guardsmen served side-by-side with Army soldiers.

This is a very basic overview of the military, intended to provide a starting point. To learn more, go to the Department of Defense website, www.defense.mil. You can click on the About tab, and then click on "DoD 101" in the drop-down menu. Here you'll find an abundance of information on the military, as well as verified links to each service branch, the National Guard, and the Reserves.

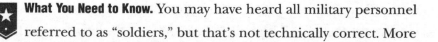 **What You Need to Know.** You may have heard all military personnel referred to as "soldiers," but that's not technically correct. More

accurate terms are "service members" or "military personnel" when referring to the military as a whole and not a specific service branch.

In the language of the military, men and women who serve in the Army are "soldiers." In the Navy, they're "sailors," while Air Force personnel are "airmen." The Marine Corps has "Marines" (yes, "Marines" is capitalized), and the Coast Guard has "Coast Guardsmen" (it's also capitalized). Likewise, the National Guard has "Guardsmen." Using the correct term goes a long way with Gold Star parents, for the proper use of soldier, sailor, airman, Marine, or Coast Guardsman is a part of their child's identity. And for the record, it matters to active-duty service members, veterans, and military families, too.

CASUALTY ASSISTANCE PROCESS

When a service member has died on active duty, casualty assistance is provided to immediate family members, those who are the legal next of kin. By definition, there is the primary next of kin, often referred to as PNOK, who is the person most closely related to the service member. For example, if the service member was married, then the surviving spouse is the primary next of kin, and the surviving parents are secondary next of kin, or SNOK. However, if the service member was unmarried and childless, then the parents are primary next of kin.

You'll probably hear the terms *primary* and *secondary next of kin* time and again, because the order of next of kin is a determining factor in making official casualty notifications, making decisions on funeral arrangements and interment, and determining eligibility for benefits.

Casualty assistance officers are assigned to primary and secondary next of kin. If the service member's parents are divorced, then each parent will have a casualty assistance officer. The titles for casualty assistance officers differ slightly among the service branches, but the duties are essentially the same.

Casualty Officer's Duties and Responsibilities

The first duty of casualty assistance personnel is to notify immediate family members. Uniformed casualty personnel officially representing the deceased member's service branch will notify the primary next of kin in person. Once the primary next of kin has been notified, in-person notifications are made to secondary next of kin. The Army and Air Force use separate teams to make notifications, and then casualty officers assume their duties. In the Navy, Marine Corps, and Coast Guard, the assigned casualty officer is part of the notification team.

The casualty assistance officer is the primary point of contact for the family with the military in the days, weeks, and months after the service member's death.

The casualty assistance officer is the primary point of contact for the family with the military in the days, weeks, and months after the service member's death. After the official notification, the casualty assistance officer provides compassionate, knowledgeable assistance to the next of kin in variety of ways:

- Coordinates the return and processing of the service member's remains.
- Helps the family make funeral and interment arrangements.
- Arranges for military funeral honors.
- Arranges for funeral travel and lodging.
- Interacts with the public affairs office on publicity requests.
- Assists with personal affairs related to the immediate family or the deceased service member.
- Reviews the eligible survivor benefits and entitlements with the next of kin and helps with processing the required paperwork.

- Apprises the next of kin of available support and assistance resources for surviving military families.
- Helps the next of kin to file a Freedom of Information Act request to obtain copies of the autopsy and other released investigative reports.

Most casualty assistance officers view their casualty service as a sacred honor and try their best to get it right—for the nation, for the uniform they wear, but most of all for their deceased brother- or sister-

Most casualty assistance officers view their casualty service as a sacred honor and try their best to get it right ...

in-arms and the surviving family members.

When the casualty process is completed, the casualty officer returns to his or her primary duties. Those parents who have had a particularly good relationship with their casualty officer often find this departure is another loss for them.

THE GOLD STAR

Few Americans recognize a gold star as a symbol of military loss, yet its history dates back to World War I, more than one hundred years ago. In 1918, President Woodrow Wilson approved the use of a gold star on a black mourning armband that was favored by mothers of that era who had lost a son in the war. The gold star quickly became the powerful symbol of the ultimate sacrifice made by service members in wartime.

In 1947, two years after World War II, Congress authorized the creation of a Gold Star Lapel Pin for family members whose loved ones died in combat, and in 1973, a second lapel pin was approved for the families of service members who died while honorably serving, but not in combat. Gold Star family members often wear these Gold Star Lapel Pins as a symbol of military loss, great pride, and a shared grief.

Today the term "Gold Star" has evolved into a general identifier of surviving family members who have lost a military member in service to our country, in times of both war and peace.

POPULAR MISCONCEPTIONS ON MILITARY LOSS

Gold Star family members often wear these Gold Star Lapel Pins as a symbol of military loss, great pride, and a shared grief.

Perhaps it is because so few Americans have experience with the military, but there are two popular, widespread beliefs about military loss that are incorrect. The first belief is that service members only die in war; the second is that military families are prepared for the loss of their loved one. Both are not true.

As a relative, friend, or service provider of a Gold Star parent, you want to be crystal clear on why these two popular beliefs are incorrect. Let's look at each one in greater detail.

1. **Service members only die in war.** Since America's earliest days, wars have claimed more than one million military personnel. These war deaths embody the ultimate sacrifice, for service members have lost their lives in the active defense and protection of our rights, freedoms, and homeland. However, war isn't the only time or circumstance in which military personnel die in the line of duty.

   Military service is a dangerous profession for all who serve, and each day approximately three service members die on active duty at home and abroad. Apart from combat and war, service members also lose their lives on other military operations; in protection of our national interests; on peacekeeping missions; from terrorist attacks at home or abroad; in maintaining operational readiness; on training exercises; from equipment failure; because of accidents; by suicide or homicide; or as a result of illness or disease.

Since the majority of these deaths go unreported in the news media, few know of the regularity with which service members die in the line of duty or that each death is a loss to our nation.

2. **Military families are prepared for the loss of their service member.** It is as difficult to explain as it is to understand, but military families are never prepared for that "knock on the door" and the bad news that follows.

... military families are never prepared for that "knock on the door" and the bad news that follows.

Today's military families are well aware that military service is often dangerous, especially if their loved one is in a combat theater of operations or a high-risk field such as special operations, aviation, or ordnance disposal. While families know full well there's a possibility their service member could be injured or killed, they also know there's a greater probability their loved one will come home safely. After all, their loved ones are professionals—part of the best military organization in the world. And with this comes confidence in their ability to do their jobs expertly, with the right training and equipment and the guidance of a highly capable and principled leadership.

That's not to say the risks of military service are ignored. Pragmatically, military personnel are required to give a DNA sample, list their next of kin, identify emergency points of contact, and designate beneficiaries for the death gratuity. Service members are also strongly encouraged to keep their life insurance beneficiaries current, particularly after life changes such as marriage or divorce, as well as to draw up a last will and testament.

On the personal level, some military families do have the "what if" conversation; others do not or cannot go there. But this is true in families outside the military as well. Even if this conversation does occur, it cannot prepare loved ones for the death of their service member. I know this from personal experience.

The mothers and fathers, spouses and children, and all others who are proud to call themselves a military family are not immune from worrying about their service member, but they always anticipate a safe return—not that "knock on the door."

While families know full well there's a possibility their service member could be injured or killed, they also know there's a greater probability their loved one will come home safely.

THE PERFECT STORM OF MILITARY GRIEF

For Gold Star parents, their grief is built upon the intersection of three powerful circumstances:

- The death of their son or daughter.
- The likelihood that death was sudden and unexpected.
- The multifaceted elements that military service brings to death.

Each of these circumstances presents daunting challenges in grief; the point where they intersect often creates the perfect storm of grief for many parents. This perfect storm has the power to unleash a formidable grief, one that has been described as raw, intense, and, at times, extreme.

In *How to Go on Living when Someone You Love Dies*, psychologist Therese Rando writes, "Parental grief is particularly intense. It is unusually complicated and has extraordinary up-and-down periods. It appears to be the most long-lasting grief of all."

As a relative, friend, or service provider, you can expect a wide range of grief reactions in the parents you interact with. While some of these reactions may seem extreme in comparison with other reactions to loss, they may be viewed as within a normal range for surviving parents.

Life will never be the same for Gold Star parents. How could it? Like most major storms, this perfect storm packs a powerful wallop. The death of a child is life changing, regardless of whether the child is an infant or a married adult in uniform. Life will never be the same for Gold Star parents. How could it?

There are seven things you need to know about Gold Star parents and this "perfect storm" of grief:

1. **Their son or daughter was young.** It's been said that military service is a young man's—and now a young woman's—game, and Gold Star parents understand the consequences of this all too well. There's a good chance their child was under thirty years old when the death occurred, and under twenty-five if that child was enlisted. While there's no good age for any child to die, many of these service members were young adults, some just barely out of their teens. They were in that life-creating, not life-ending, time of life. This adds to making the death harder to accept.

2. **Their child was a part of something greater than themselves.** Military service has an important purpose in our troubled world, from keeping the peace to protecting America from bad guys looking to do us harm. In spite of the risks, the sons and daughters of Gold Star parents volunteered to serve our country. In their short lives, they made contributions to the greater good and had the potential to contribute much more.

Gold Star parents lost not only a child in whom they took great pride, but also a valuable member of society. America was robbed of the promise and potential that these service members possessed.

3. **Their child may have died a sudden death far from home.** Because of war, military operations, deployments, or duty stations abroad, service members frequently die away from American soil. When the loss occurs far from home, Gold Star parents find themselves in an impossible predicament. When a child of any age dies, it's common for parental instincts to kick in, and military parents are no exception. Shocked by the sudden and unexpected death of their child, they're also isolated by where they live geographically, the distance to where their child died, time zone changes, lack of initial details, and their legal status as the primary or secondary next of kin.

> *Gold Star parents lost not only a child in whom they took great pride, but also a valuable member of society.*

When a child of any age is in crisis, it's difficult for a parent to sit and wait. Gold Star parents often feel helpless—unable to help their child when they want to the most. They must rely on others during what is unquestionably the worst tragedy of their lives.

4. **How their child died impacts the surviving parents.** For Gold Star parents, the suddenness of their child's death influences how they initially react to the news, while the cause of death impacts what they will cope with in the months and years to come.

How the service member died can have a lasting effect on parents, as some military deaths are traumatic in nature, both in and outside of combat and war. A sudden death, how it happened, and the condition of the remains all contribute to the depth and duration of grief for Gold Star parents.

Earlier in this chapter, you read that service members die each day with unnoticed regularity. When a service member dies in circumstances other than combat, this loss is sometimes viewed as less important or relevant to the nation. When this occurs, Gold Star parents find that the loss of their child may not be fully recognized, and they may not get the support they need. Their child's death—as well as their grief—may be disenfranchised by those around them. This adds another complication to their grief journey.

5. **The casualty assistance process is traumatic.** For some parents, the casualty assistance team may be their first interaction with uniformed military personnel, apart from their child and his or her friends. Casualty assistance is an undeniably unnerving process, from the first glimpse of the uniformed military personnel at the door to the heartbreaking news they brought with them. It's common for parents to remember where, when, and how they were told "the news," for this moment is burned into their memory. And it is one that can be recalled in an instant with vivid clarity. Without question, actual notification of the death is a traumatic event, but it's only the beginning of the casualty process.

Once notification is made, it's followed by support from the casualty assistance officer. If the parents are the primary next of kin or were authorized by their child to handle the funeral and burial arrangements, the casualty officer works closely with them. Planning a child's funeral is an incomprehensible and heartbreaking task.

Casualty assistance doesn't end with the funeral. The full
scope of casualty support will, once again, depend on the
service member's marital status. One decision that's unique to
military loss is how the service member's personal effects are
returned. If the service member was deployed, their personal
possessions are neatly boxed up and shipped home. Before
this begins, the casualty officer will ask the next of kin whether
they want the service member's clothes laundered or they want
the clothes sent home "as is." While this may seem an odd
question to some who are reading this chapter, parents often
choose to have the clothes sent home unwashed in the hope
they'll still smell like their child. And if they're fortunate to get
back clothing that has their child's recognizable odor, it will be
handled like a precious family heirloom.

Depending upon the next-of-kin status of the parents, the
bulk of the casualty process may last for thirty to forty-five days,
with stray details and needs popping up for months to come.

6. **Military funerals leave a lifelong mark on hearts and souls.** When
parents or the surviving spouse opt for a military funeral,
the service member receives military funeral honors.
These honors are America's way of paying respect to a
service member or veteran who has honorably served. It
is a profound and powerful tribute, and its traditions and
rituals form a lasting, powerful memory for all who witness
it: the flag-draped casket, a rifle salute, the haunting notes
of "Taps," and the official presentation of the folded casket
flag to the family with the words "On behalf of the president
of the United States, the [United States Army; United States
Navy; United States Marine Corps; United States Air Force;
or United States Coast Guard], and a grateful nation, please

accept this flag as a symbol of our appreciation for your loved one's honorable and faithful service."

The power of a military funeral remains long after the service concludes. Gold Star parents quickly learn how deeply military service and its traditions are woven into the fabric of our culture. Perhaps unnoticed in the parents' "old life" before the death, newspapers and magazines are filled with poignant images of service and sacrifice, particularly around Memorial Day and Veterans Day. Scenes of military funerals and moving tributes pop up often in movies and television shows. For parents, each occurrence is a personal, and sometimes painful, reminder of their loss. While the uneasiness of coming across scenes such as these diminishes over time, images of military funerals will never be impersonal for Gold Star parents.

7. **Gold Star parents contend with a dual loss that few understand.** The majority of Gold Star parents are hardworking moms and dads, usually living and working in communities across the land. Like many who are reading these chapters, they know little about military loss or what lies ahead for them.

Gold Star parents sometimes feel isolated by their loss—outsiders looking in on the military and alone in their own civilian communities. The very nature of their loss may cause families and friends to unintentionally stay away. Sometimes it's easier to feel guilty from a distance than to be uncomfortable in the presence of Gold Star parents.

Gold Star parents regularly face private and public reminders of their loss. For example, they strongly identify with the American flag and all that it represents, as it becomes a personal connection to their child's life, purpose, and loss.

Gold Star parents have been known to take offense when the flag is disrespected; you will find most parents are patriotic, protective, and emotional about America, both in and out of the public spotlight.

As mentioned previously, our country has two federal holidays dedicated to service members, both living and deceased. Memorial Day, observed on the last Monday of May, honors the servicemen and -women who have fought and died in war and also those who have died while honorably serving in the armed forces. Veterans Day, always observed on November 11, honors all veterans who have proudly served, both living and deceased.

You also need to know and pass on this fact: it's never a good idea to wish a Gold Star parent a "Happy" Memorial Day.

For a large chunk of the population, Memorial Day is commonly seen as a three-day weekend and the unofficial start of summer. For Gold Star parents, it takes on personal meaning, for their child is now among the fallen who are honored and remembered. You need to know that Gold Star parents are sensitive about how Memorial Day has been commercialized into a long holiday weekend, usually chock-full of sales events and backyard get-togethers. All too often, its intended purpose of honoring the fallen goes unnoticed. You also need to know and pass on this fact: it's never a good idea to wish a Gold Star parent a "Happy" Memorial Day.

What You Need to Know. A good deal of information is presented in this chapter, and it will likely take you more than one reading to digest it. But it's worth that second read. If you remember nothing else from this chapter, the following points are important to keep in mind:

1. Parents are never prepared for that "knock on the door" and the bad news that follows.
2. Service members die in peacetime as well as in war.
3. The perfect storm of military grief packs a powerful wallop.
4. Military grief is complex, complicated, and just plain messy.
5. It's never a good idea to wish Gold Star parents a "Happy" Memorial Day.

CHAPTER 15

What to Expect

I'll always remember the day I graduated from high school. On the way home from the ceremony, our family car was broadsided by a Volvo—you know, one of those old models that was built like a tank. It happened without warning, and no one in the car saw it coming.

My family and I were all banged up. My right leg was pretty messed up, bleeding and broken below the knee. I'd never been injured like that before and had no clue what to expect.

I hurt from head to toe, if you'll pardon the pun. About six months later, the doctor pronounced me "as good as new." But I really wasn't. My leg was never the same. It ached and hurt at the strangest times. Even now, some fifty years later, my leg often reminds me of how badly it was damaged. I've learned to live with it.

In my own way, this is how I'd describe the grief I felt after my son was killed. Only that injury was a thousand times worse.

Mark (Oklahoma)

We live in a world that's largely removed from death and grief. While we're more exposed to horrific tragedies in this digital age, these deaths usually don't touch us personally, nor does the grief that burdens its survivors. Even in our own families, many of which are scattered across the country, we often have less exposure to the death of relatives, have less opportunity to attend their funerals, and are less likely to feel the weight of their loss. As a result, we don't have much experience with grief and know little about it. It's a subject that's easily avoided.

Many Americans have some preconceived ideas about military loss. Perhaps because of the public nature of some military losses or how they are reported in the media, general assumptions exist on how service members die, who makes up the surviving family, and how these family members should conduct themselves.

All too often the realities of military loss don't match up with the public perception of it. This is particularly true with military loss when personal grief is likely to cross paths with patriotism and publicity.

It's safe to say that you don't know what to expect from grief, particularly this military variety. Neither do the Gold Star parents. Even though they're living with this grief, it's largely unknown to them.

You already know that being with parents who have lost a child can be uncomfortable. To help ease this possible discomfort, what to expect when a parent has lost a son or daughter in the line of duty will be reviewed. As a reminder, this material may be hard to read, for the death of a child is a particularly sobering subject, one that can push buttons within you, if it hasn't already.

In the previous chapter, you read about the perfect storm of military grief. In this chapter, what grief is and the many ways it can affect the parents will be examined.

GRIEF

In its simplest form, grief is a natural and expected reaction to loss, but one that's hard to put into words. Even though grief is a worldwide occurrence, there's no one-size-fits-all definition that works for everyone. Multiple factors influence grief, making it a deeply personal and separate experience for each parent. While Gold Star parents share the loss of a child, the personal grief they experience will be different for each parent.

While Gold Star parents share the loss of a child, the personal grief they experience will be different for each parent.... it's just plain wrong for a child to die first.

The previous paragraph describes grief as a natural reaction to loss, but there's nothing natural about the death of a son or daughter. It's a profound and devastating loss, regardless of whether the child is an infant, a teenager, or a married adult in uniform. And it's just plain wrong for a child to die first.

GRIEF IS A PACKAGE DEAL

When you think about grief, more often than not tears and visible sadness come to mind. While these reactions are recognized as part of grief, they're only a small component of its makeup.

Grief has multiple dimensions and affects parents in some surprising and unpredictable ways. For many parents, grief will have an effect on their physical health in addition to the emotional upheaval they endure. Grief can also compromise their ability to remember details, think clearly, or make decisions. It can be seen in how a parent behaves and interacts with others. And it often causes parents to question their understanding of life and death and the way the world works—or, in their case, the way the world should have worked. What does this mean? It means that grief has the power to affect body, mind, and spirit.

Grief is a perplexing web of thoughts, behaviors, emotions, and feelings. Unfortunately, parents can't choose one reaction over another. Grief comes as a package deal.

Emotional Reactions

You will find some parents display visible emotional reactions, such as keening, tears, or the look of someone who carries the weight of the world on his or her shoulders. But not every parent is outwardly emotional. Some Gold Star parents cry without tears, keeping their emotions in check. For others, their emotions come out as irritability, anger, or guilt, to name just a few reactions.

Behavioral Reactions

Behaviors aren't actions you would normally connect with grief, but it's a way grief comes out in some parents. Sometimes, parents release their pent-up anxiety and feelings of grief in physical ways.

If your gut instinct is saying something isn't right—listen to it.

Acting out expressions of grief can be positive, such as when it's channeled into manual labor, a project, or a high-energy sport. It can also be as simple as beating up a pillow.

Acting out can also be negative, when the actions are high risk, harmful, or destructive to the grieving parent or those who come in contact with him or her.

Be on the lookout for signs of excessive alcohol or substance abuse, child or spousal abuse, recklessness, or any behaviors that cause you concern. If your gut instinct is saying something isn't right—listen to it.

Physical Reactions

Physical reactions are another dimension of grief. Know that grief is a powerful stressor and can affect a parent's body in obvious and not-so-obvious ways. Fatigue, exhaustion, back and neck pain, and insomnia are commonly associated with grief, along with a host of other physical symptoms. Grief can also weaken the immune system, causing parents to easily get sick. It can also ignite a flare-up of a prior medical or mental health condition. Grief isn't picky about what it affects.

Be on the alert for physical changes in parents and encourage them to get medical attention. It's not uncommon for some parents to adopt an "I don't care" attitude after a loss.

Cognitive Reactions

Grief often has a field day with a parent's ability to think clearly, concentrate, remember details, or make decisions.

Grief often has a field day with a parent's ability to think clearly, concentrate, remember details, or make decisions. This can be frustrating for parents, especially when they realize they're struggling with mental tasks they once did without a second thought. It can also be frustrating for those around them. You can help them stay on track with friendly reminders of appointments and other time-sensitive needs.

Social Reactions

The social reactions of grief may not be immediately obvious, as parents often receive a lot of attention immediately after their child's death. Around the three-month mark, this attention drops off and parents usually find they're on their own for the first time since their loss. Don't expect parents to jump back into their old routines. They may lose interest in activities they once were active in. Some parents will withdraw, while others may find ways to constantly be away from their homes.

Spiritual Reactions

The spiritual side of grief is powerful, but it's often overlooked as a dimension of grief. Spirituality means different things to different people. For some parents, spirituality may stand on its own as a way of making sense of their loss; for others it's an integral part of their religious beliefs. Parents have said the death of their child upset the natural cycle of life, which challenged their existing beliefs on life, death, and the fairness of the world. Some parents may become angry with the God they believe in, while others turn to their religious beliefs for comfort and the way to search for answers to some of life's toughest questions.

Not every parent will experience all the grief dimensions found here. Grief is uniquely personal. Some reactions may dominate one parent's grieving style, but not be experienced by another. You can anticipate an assortment of reactions and responses in parents, sometimes within a short amount of time. It's not uncommon for a parent to be angry one minute and visibly emotional the next. Grief can be unpredictable.

DIFFERENT GRIEVING STYLES

Earlier in this chapter, you read that there's no one-size-fits-all definition for grief. Just as grief can't be packaged into one neat and tidy description, there's also no right or wrong way to grieve. As a relative *... there is no* or friend of a Gold Star parent, you need to know *and* *right or wrong* remember this important fact: there is no right or wrong *way to grieve.* way to grieve.

In today's America, we tend to hold onto the deep-rooted belief that genuine grief is predominately emotional, and these emotions are displayed and shared with others. Few realize that emotions are only one way to grieve. For some mothers and fathers, strongly displayed emotions are not how they respond to tragedy and loss.

Some Gold Star parents grieve intuitively, experiencing grief as feelings, some of which can be intense or overwhelming. These parents need to feel the pain of grief and talk about it, often finding comfort and strength in sharing their grief, particularly with other parents who can relate to military loss.

Other Gold Star parents are instrumental grievers. They also experience the pain of grief, but strive to keep their emotions under control. Instrumental grievers work to redirect their emotional energy into actions. Some parents prefer not to talk about their feelings, but may gravitate to issues brought on by the loss and work to resolve them. They like to solve problems.

... the differences in how Gold Star parents grieve are not differences in how much they loved their son or daughter.

When instrumental parents aren't taking action, they're comfortable handling grief intellectually, tending to think their way through it. These parents may be uncomfortable around others who are openly emotional. You can anticipate a blend of both styles in parents.

As a relative, friend, or service provider, try to set aside that ingrained belief that all grief should be felt, displayed, and shared by emotional reactions. As you've read in this chapter, grief is experienced in many forms, and it's not necessary for every parent to "let it all out" as they cope with their loss. But the differences in how Gold Star parents grieve are not differences in how much they loved their son or daughter.

LENGTH OF GRIEF

There is a common, but incorrect, belief that after a death it takes about a year to "get over it"—whatever that means. Know with certainty that "get over it" is not a part of a Gold Star parent's vocabulary. You can count on a Gold Star parent's grief to stick around for the rest of his or her life in some shape or form.

It will probably take longer than you would imagine for parents to work through grief's toughest parts. But don't be fooled into thinking that once the intensity of it lessens, they're finished with grief. It doesn't work that way. Grief doesn't unfold in an orderly or predictable way, and you'll find that parents revisit issues time and

Grief has no respect for progress. Don't expect parents to bounce back to their "old selves" again, for those "old selves" disappeared the day their child died.

again. This unpredictability is a normal part of the process. Grief has no respect for progress.

While the parent's grief should lessen in intensity, some level of grief will remain with him or her. Don't expect parents to bounce back to their "old selves" again, for those "old selves" disappeared the day their child died.

SECONDARY LOSSES

In the months and years to come, Gold Star parents will experience additional losses stemming directly from the death of their son or daughter. Called secondary losses, these additional losses generate more pain and heartache, and also genuine grief.

For instance, parents who have lost an only child must cope with never being called Mom or Dad again. And down the road, these same parents face another major loss when their relatives and friends become grandparents and they're denied this opportunity because of their child's death. Be mindful that when parents experience secondary losses, they are again burdened with the seemingly endless ramifications arising out of their child's death. And because of that death, they often feel that more things they cherish have been taken away from them. And they have no control over stopping it.

MILITARY GRIEF HAS A LONG SHELF LIFE

Earlier in this book, you read that a military death often has "add-ons," those complicating factors usually not found in civilian deaths. And because of those factors, it may seem that parents move slowly through their grief, often taking two steps forward, then one step backward. This is true; nothing about grief is straightforward.

Here, we'll look at a few additional factors that can add years to military grief's shelf life.

Denial

It's unwise to assume that just because parents have been officially notified, they unconditionally believe that their child is dead. Early on, the nature of military loss may hamper a parent's ability to acknowledge and internalize this news. Without forewarning, parents are faced with their child's sudden death, an official notification but one without hands-on proof, and the inability to go to the scene of the death and "see with their own eyes." You may wonder if the parents' inability to fully acknowledge their child's death is a form of denial, but others see it as a reality of military loss.

Lingering Doubts

More that 80 percent of military deaths are sudden, and some are violent in nature, causing significant damage to the body. Viewing the remains may be impossible, denying parents the visual proof that their child is dead. Even with DNA confirmation, but without this eyes-on proof, parents may have lingering doubts that the remains in the casket are those of their child. Down the road, you may encounter parents who regret that they didn't press the issue and view even a small portion of their child's remains. This regret is more common than not, and those doubts may last a lifetime.

Deployment-Delayed Grief

If the service member died on deployment, in war, or on an extended military operation, a surviving parent may find it harder to believe the news, especially if a closed casket was necessary or no body was recovered. After all, their child was *supposed* to be away. And when that deployment ended, it's not uncommon for parents to hold onto a glimmer of hope that—just maybe—the Department of Defense had made a mistake and their child would be coming home with the rest of the returning forces.

You can expect parents to face a sobering dose of reality when the forces come home without their child, extinguishing that last glimmer of hope they held onto that their child may still be alive. Called *deployment-delayed grief,* this dose of reality can unleash heightened grief reactions in parents, sometimes as painful as their early reactions to the news of the death.

Doses of Reality

It takes about a year or more for the reality of any sudden death to sink in. Encountering reality is a painful process for Gold Star parents, for each dose of it teaches them again that their son or daughter is dead. It's been said that the first million doses of reality are the hardest.

Reality is often rude, waiting for parents in a variety of people, places, and things. And for Gold Star parents, reality is both public and private. National symbols of our country often become personal reminders of their loss, a fact that's often hard for nonsurvivors to understand. As an example, for the majority of Americans, our flag is a respected symbol, often evoking feelings of pride, patriotism, and love of country. For Gold Star parents those feelings take on a deeper meaning, for this revered symbol of America once draped their child's casket. A flag-draped casket is a memory that never fades away, and it's impossible for Gold Star parents to separate the flag from thoughts of their child.

It's been said that the first million doses of reality are the hardest.

The painful lessons of reality are also private: an unopened jar of their son's favorite peanut butter in the cabinet, an old birthday card in their daughter's handwriting, or their grandson calling another man "Dad." Parents have their own personal list of moments of reality, and each and every one reminds them that their child is dead. These doses of reality are painful, and their cumulative effect often seems never-ending.

Obsession with Details

You read in an earlier paragraph that most military deaths are sudden and traumatic. With these deaths, it would be a common, and even expected, part of the grief process for parents to want a clear understanding of the events that led up to their child's death, the details surrounding it, and what happened afterward.

The casualty officer provides the factual details that are a part of the notification, but that's *never* enough information. Additional details may be found in after-action reports and investigations, but these findings take time—often weeks, sometimes months, and occasionally years. In the meantime, unofficial accounts, rumors, and innuendos abound, and parents will try to piece together all that they hear from different sources. Knowing how and why their child died is a powerful need for parents, and that need to know may last a lifetime.

Parents will tell—and retell—the story of how their child died as they internally put the pieces together. You may find this obsession with the death details to be somewhat morbid, but don't be tempted to discourage them. Initially, it's a critical element of their attempt to make sense of the death, and later, it becomes a part of their search for meaning in their child's life and death. It's been my experience that Gold Star family members, myself included, can tell the story of how our loved ones died, in exacting detail, even decades later.

Bumps in the Road

As a relative or friend, you will hope to see progress in parents, signs that they are "doing so much better." What you won't like to see are those bad days, when grief shows up in full force. The truth about grief is that the journey through it is never smooth sailing. There isn't a GPS for grief that will guide the parents around the detours and obstacles that are a part of their grief journey.

Gold Star parents deal with all the stressors that are present whenever a child dies. They are also faced with particular bumps in the road that are part of their military grief. These bumps are unknowns, in both their nature and their way of arrival, and can result in bursts of grief for them. A few bumps in the road are:

- Arrival of their child's footlocker, seabag, clothing, and other personal possessions from a deployment location or duty station several months down the road.
- Return of previously mailed packages and letters stamped with "Deceased."
- Release of investigations, final reports, and autopsy results months after the death.
- News of other military deaths, particularly those similar to their child's.
- Memorial Day ceremonies and the lack of respect for Memorial Day.
- Attacks on America, the military, and the flag.

Bumps in the road—in all shapes and forms—will be around for a lifetime. Some may produce strong reactions in parents, even years down the road. This doesn't mean parents haven't dealt with their loss; it simply means the scars from their loss will always be sensitive spots for them. Love, loss, and grief are like that.

What You Need to Know. There is more good information to chew on in this chapter, and many of its points will be invaluable at different times in a Gold Star parent's life. If you remember nothing else from this chapter, this is what you need to know:

1. It is just plain wrong for a child to die first.
2. There is no one right or wrong way to grieve.

3. Grief has the power to affect the body, mind, and spirit.

4. Know with certainty that "get over it" is not a part of a Gold Star parent's vocabulary.

5. If your gut instinct is saying that something isn't right—listen to it.

CHAPTER 16

What to Say and Do

I'm learning the hard way that I make people uncomfortable. It's not that I deliberately try to do so, but I can feel it in how they treat me. It's only been ten months since Duane was killed, and there are days when I want to scream, "I've lost my son! I don't want to be cheered up or pumped full of hope for a better tomorrow."

I live with the unspeakable pain that comes from losing a child. I ask only that you patiently tolerate me as I make this journey through grief. And please, don't turn away from me.

Laura (Washington)

When you are with parents who have lost a son or daughter in the military, you may feel a greater need to say and do all the right things, whether it's at the time of the funeral or memorial service or months down the road when you run into them at your local convenience store. You're not alone. Most people struggle with this.

It's important to keep in mind that when talking with Gold Star parents, you're dealing with two sets of emotions: those of the grieving parents and your own feelings as well. How you respond will depend on:

- How well you know the parents.
- How well (or if) you knew the service member.
- How the service member died.
- Amount of time since the death.
- How uneasy you're feeling.

Your own uneasy feelings can impact what you say. Like most people in these delicate circumstances, you want to say something meaningful, but may be at a loss for words. You may also struggle with how badly you feel for the parents; perhaps you feel the need to help ease their pain. And if you are a parent, you may be personally uncomfortable witnessing the grief over losing a son or daughter.

Viewings, funerals, or memorial services are a time to publicly grieve and mourn for the surviving parents, relatives, and friends, as well as all who are present.

Military loss pushes buttons in all of us. All too often, the collective anxieties of the moment can take center stage and—even with the best of intentions—what you say doesn't come out as you intended. It happens to the best of us.

To help you become better prepared, how to say and do the right things early on, and then later down the road, will be discussed.

EARLY ON

Viewings, funerals, or memorial services are a time to publicly grieve and mourn for the surviving parents, relatives, and friends, as well as all who are present. There's no denying these are emotionally charged events, but you can offer your personal condolences in meaningful ways. Based on the wisdom found in years of lessons learned, here are a few tips to keep in mind.

Nine Tips for Offering Condolences

1. When you talk with parents, look directly at them, speak clearly, and be loud enough to be heard. Don't rush your words. If you're comfortable with offering a human touch, take their hand or give them a hug.

    What You Need to Know. Sometimes, when people are nervous or uncomfortable, they tend to avoid eye contact or mumble. Try not to be one of those people.

2. Be sincere, compassionate, and brief. It's not necessary to be long-winded to get your message across.

3. A good statement of condolence is "I'm sorry for your loss." A better one is "I'm sorry for the loss of your son or daughter." (You've identified the lost relationship.)

4. The best is "I'm sorry for the loss of your son, Jayden, or your daughter, Amber." (You've personalized it by using their child's name.)

5. If you feel the need to say more, a good follow-up is "Thank you for raising a good son or daughter." And "Please accept my sympathy" works, too.

6. After you've offered your condolences, it's okay to stop talking.

7. There may be times when you truly don't know what to say. If that's the case, then simply say, "I don't know what to say," or "I'm at a loss for words."

8. Try not to use the phrase "You're in my thoughts and prayers." While it may be a heartfelt message, it's used so often it's beginning to sound clichéd.

9. Share a quick memory if you knew the service member. Parents will love to hear stories about their child, since telling a good story focuses on the life, rather than on the death.

What You Need to Know. Try not to use the term "passed away" with military loss, as this phrase has the connotation of a peaceful, anticipated death. Since most military deaths are sudden and sometimes violent, they are better identified with "died" or "killed." Language matters here. "My son was killed in the line of duty" has a much different meaning from "My daughter passed away while she was in the Army."

With a few tips on what to say under your belt, it's time to look at what not to say.

WHAT NOT TO SAY

When you're with surviving parents, it's often a natural instinct to try to make them feel better or offer hope for better days ahead. But that's not what parents need to hear, especially at the viewing, memorial, or funeral for their child, for these services are times of shared grief and mourning.

Here's a list of what not to say to Gold Star parents—or anyone who has lost someone close. As you read through it, you'll notice phrases that have become the go-to remarks for offering condolences. No matter how well-intentioned many of them sound, these phrases all have one thing in common: none offer expressions of sympathy.

- "Time heals all wounds."
- "I know exactly how you feel."
- "I don't know how I'd survive in your shoes."
- "I'm happy you have other children."
- "I'm glad you had your son [or daughter] for as long as you did."
- "It was God's will."
- "God never gives us more than we can handle."

- "Everything happens for a reason."
- "Cherish your memories."
- "Don't dwell on his [or her] death. Remember the happy times."
- "It was his [or her] time to go."
- "Your child is happy where he [or she] is."
- "You've got to move on with your life."

HOW THESE PHRASES MAY BE HEARD

No one intends to say anything inappropriate to surviving parents. But many of these phrases have become so ingrained in our conversations that little thought is given to their meaning or how they sound to parents who hear them.

Do parents find comfort in these phrases? Probably not. It's not uncommon for parents to feel many of them minimize their loss. Some sound unsympathetic. For example, a mother may be told, "I'm happy you have other children," and want to cry out, "I love all my children, but I lost a child. No other child will ever fill that void." Likewise, a father may be told, "It was her time to go," and internally protest, "It wasn't her time. And it definitely wasn't my time for her to go."

★ **Point to Remember.** Consider mentally rehearsing what you plan to say. As you do, ask yourself this question: *Would it make me feel better?*

HOW TO HELP EARLY ON

Once parents are officially notified, all other parts of their lives get put on hold. They usually receive a lot of support early on, but it drops off dramatically after the funeral or memorial. Now more than ever, they could use a helping hand as they're likely in survival mode and, more often than not, physically as well as emotionally exhausted.

If you would like to help in the weeks after the funeral, a good way to start is by offering practical help, starting with the "stuff" that was put on hold and now needs attention. You can provide practical help in any number of ways that suit your available time, skills set, and personality:

- Cut the grass or shovel snow, depending upon the season.
- Sort through the mail and separate condolence cards and bills from junk mail.
- Return dishes and containers that were sent over with food.
- Run errands.
- Clean the house.
- Do laundry, especially if guests had stayed over.
- Get the car inspected, fixed, or washed.
- Reschedule appointments.
- Take care of flower arrangements sent to the parents' house.
- Make a list of all who provided help.
- Provide gift certificates or coupons for local take-out food.
- Be the "gatekeeper" and shield the parents from media and other inquiries.
- Offer to drive parents to appointments, particularly the difficult ones.
- Write out thank you cards.

Keep in mind that parents may honestly not know what they need or want, so it's okay to suggest a few ways you can help. Some may jump at your offer of assistance; others may not. But don't let a refusal of help stop you from asking again in a couple of days or weeks.

WHAT TO SAY DOWN THE ROAD

There is no statute of limitations on offering condolences. It doesn't matter whether it's been months or years down the road; if you come in contact with Gold Star parents whom you haven't seen since their loss, it's always the right thing to offer your condolences: "I'm sorry for the loss of your son/daughter (name)."

It is important that you acknowledge the loss, especially if you'll be spending time with them at social, professional, or family gatherings. Otherwise, you run the risk of having that awkward "elephant in the room," which the Merriam-Webster dictionary defines as "an obvious major problem or issue that people avoid discussing or acknowledging." When that elephant is in the room, your conversations with Gold Star parents may be a bit strained because you know they've lost a child since you've last seen them, and they know that you know. When this loss isn't acknowledged, everyone is uncomfortable.

Whether it's been ten days, ten months, or ten years since the loss, it's an instinctive reaction to ask parents how they're doing. A good way to ask is, "How are you doing *today*," or "How's it going *today*? By adding "today," it focuses your question on the here and now. The plain old "How are you doing?" encourages an automatic reply of "Fine."

HOW TO HELP DOWN THE ROAD

Being a good friend or relative to Gold Star parents is often a trial-and-error experience. Grief reactions are unpredictable. And while what you said or did may have seemed helpful one day, the next day it could produce an opposite reaction, depending on the parents' mood, external factors, or even which way the wind was blowing. Sometimes the right responses to the needs and wants of parents are hard to figure out.

Here are seven ideas on ways to support Gold Star parents down the road:

1. **Practice the 80/20 rule.** Gold Star parents need to talk about their child, especially early on. It's a healthy part of their grief to do so. Don't be surprised at the range of stories they'll tell—everything from cute baby stories to details of the death. You'll probably hear these stories more than once, and that's okay. They serve an important purpose in grief.

   Concentrate on listening 80 percent of the time and use the remaining 20 percent of talk time wisely. It's a quirk in our human nature to bring up deaths we've personally experienced in the company of those who are grieving. In all honesty, parents probably don't want to hear about your losses, unless you've also lost a child.

2. **Tell stories about their child if you have them.** One wise way to use that 20 percent of your time is to share memories of their son or daughter. Tell stories of happy times, funny times. You'll notice parents will brighten up at these stories and are usually eager to hear more. They may even tell a few of their own. Stories about their child that they haven't heard before are priceless and will likely be appreciated.

3. **Offer practical help.** Perhaps you're uncomfortable with hearing about losing a child, but would still like to help out in some way. One easy way to do so is to perform those random acts of kindness we often hear about. It can be as simple as taking in their trash cans from the curb, or placing their newspaper on their porch, or asking if they need anything from the grocery store the next time you're headed there.

4. **Remember them on their child's date of death.** Many parents feel it's a thoughtful act to hear from family and friends on the day their child died. Try not to dance around the subject in

indirect ways, such as "I wanted to reach out to you at this difficult time." Parents know full well how difficult this day is. Take the direct approach: "I'm calling today because it's the day your David died, and I wanted you to know that I remember, too." You may be the only person who remembers them, because with lightning speed, the world forgets and moves on.

5. **Reach out when similar military deaths occur.** It's a question not of if, but of when a military death will occur that's similar to their child's death. The news of this death automatically erases time for these parents and, with chilling accuracy, they'll relive their child's loss, particularly if the cause is the same or the death happened in the same unit their child served in. It's an act of kindness to reach out to these parents at this time, and they'll appreciate your thoughtful support, even if it's a quick phone call.

6. **Offer them a break from grief and a chance to reinvest in life.** Men and women handle grief in different ways, and it's sometimes a good idea to invite them separately to events they find interesting and enjoy. A father may enjoy some male bonding time, doing whatever interests the both of you. Likewise, a mother may appreciate a little girlfriend time, spending it in ways that are good for her.

   Parents benefit from time away from each other, especially with relatives or good friends with whom they can let their guard down and relax.

7. **Try not to brag (too) much about your own children.** It's natural for parents to share good news about their children. While Gold Star parents may honestly appreciate hearing this news, it

can be a double-edged sword for them. For surviving parents, it's another dose of reality, a reminder that they no longer will share good news about their child's achievements and accomplishments. If their reactions surprise you, keep in mind that it has nothing to do with you or your child.

This section has focused on helping Gold Star parents. Now it's time to focus on how to take care of yourself. Loss and grief may take their toll on relatives and friends, and you're not immune from the emotional, physical, and spiritual weariness that often goes along with helping those who have suffered a profound loss.

In Chapter Thirteen, you'll find fourteen proven ways to maintain or increase your personal resilience. If you're like most people, you would like to have more energy. The information found in this chapter can help set in motion the means to give you additional energy every day, as well as the skills to use it more effectively.

Point to Remember. Hopefully, this chapter has helped you feel more confident and compassionate in your words and actions when you're in the company of Gold Star parents. If you remember nothing else from it, this is what you need to know:

1. There is no statute of limitations for offering condolences.
2. Look directly at Gold Star parents, speak clearly, and be loud enough to be heard when you're offering condolences.
3. Avoid many of the standard condolence clichés.
4. The language of death matters. Use "died" or "killed" when it's appropriate, rather than "passed away."
5. Loss and grief take their toll on relatives and friends, too. Actively take care of yourself.

Bibliography

Barak, Adi, and Ronit D. Leichtentritt. "Ideological Meaning Making after the Loss of a Child: The Case of Israeli Bereaved Parents." *Death Studies* 39, no. 6 (2015), 360–68.

Baugher, Bob. *Understanding Guilt During Bereavement.* Baugher, 2008.

Baugher, Bob, and Jack Jordan. *After Suicide Loss: Coping with Your Grief.* Baugher and Jordan, 2002.

Bellet, Benjamin W., Robert A. Neimeyer, and Jeffrey S. Berman. "Event Centrality and Bereavement Symptomatology." *OMEGA: Journal of Death and Dying* (2016), 003022281667965. doi:10.1177/0030222816667965.

Boss, Pauline, Lorraine Beaulieu, Elizabeth Wieling, William Turner, and Shulaika LaCruz. "Healing Loss, Ambiguity, and Trauma: A Community-Based Intervention with Families of Union Workers Missing after the 9/11 Attack in New York City." *Journal of Marital and Family Therapy* (2003): 455–67.

Bruce, Elizabeth J., and Cynthia L. Schultz. *Nonfinite Loss and Grief.* Baltimore: Paul H. Brookes Publishing Co., 2001.

Calhoun, Lawrence G., Richard G. Tedeschi, Arnie Cann, and Emily A. Hanks. "Positive Outcomes Following Bereavement: Paths to Posttraumatic Growth." *Psychologica Belgica* 50, no. 1-2 (2010), 125.

Carroll, Bonnie, and Alan D. Wolfelt. *Healing Your Grieving Heart after a Military Death: 100 Practical Ideas for Families and Friends.* Fort Collins, CO: Companion Press, 2015.

Clark, Andrew. "Working with Grieving Adults." *Advances in Psychiatric Treatment* (2004): 164–70.

Cozza, Stephen J., Joscelyn E. Fisher, Christine Mauro, Jing Zhou, Claudio D. Ortiz, Natalia Skritskaya, Melanie M. Wall, Carol S. Fullerton, Robert J. Ursano, and M. K. Shear. "Performance of *DSM-5* Persistent Complex Bereavement Disorder Criteria in a Community Sample of Bereaved Military Family Members." *American Journal of Psychiatry* 173, no. 9 (2016), 919–29. doi:10.1176/appi.ajp.2016.15111442.

Cozza, Stephen J., Joscelyn E. Fisher, Jing Zhou, Jill Harrington-LaMorie, Lareina La Flair, Carol S. Fullerton, and Robert J. Ursano. "Bereaved Military Dependent Spouses and Children: Those Left Behind in a Decade of War (2001–2011)." *Military Medicine* 182, no. 3 (2017), e1684–90.

Dass-Brailsford, Priscilla. *A Practical Approach to Trauma.* Los Angeles: Thousand Oaks, 2007.

Doka, Kenneth J., ed. *Disenfranchised Grief.* Champaign, IL: Research Press, 2002.

——. *Living with Grief after Sudden Loss.* New York: Taylor & Francis, 1996.

Doka, Kenneth J., and Amy S. Tucci, eds. *Improving Care for Veterans Facing Illness and Death.* Washington, DC: Hospice Foundation of America, 2013.

——. *When Grief Is Complicated.* Washington, DC: Hospice Foundation of America, 2017.

Doka, Kenneth J., and Terry L. Martin. *Grieving Beyond Gender.* New York: Routledge, 2010.

Field, Nigel P., Wendy Packman, Rama Ronen, Angeliki Pries, Betty Davies, and Robyn Kramer. "Type of Continuing Bonds Expression and Its Comforting Versus Distressing Nature: Implications for Adjustment among Bereaved Mothers." *Death Studies* 37, no. 10 (2013), 889–912. doi:10.1080/07481187.2012.692458.

Figley, Charles R. "What Is Compassion Fatigue: Prevention & Treatment." 2012. http://giftfromwithin.org/html/What-is-Compassion-Fatigue.

Golden, Thomas R. *Swallowed by a Snake.* Gaithersburg: Golden Healing Publishing, LLC, 2000.

Harrington, Christina. "Meaning Making in Wartime Bereavement: Lessons Learned from Bereaved Parents and Siblings." *OMEGA: Journal of Death and Dying* 76, no. 2 (2016), 103–21.

Harington-LaMorie, Jill. "Operation Iraqi Freedom/Operation Enduring Freedom: Exploring Wartime Death and Bereavement." *Social Work in Health Care* 50, no. 7 (2011), 543–63. doi:10.1080/00981389.2010.532050.

Harrington-LaMorie, Jill. "Recognizing and Grieving Secondary Losses." *TAPS Magazine* (Spring 2013): 14–16.

Harrington-LaMorie, Jill and Meghan McDevitt-Murphy. "Traumatic Death in the United States Military: Initiating Dialogue on War-Related Losses." In *Grief and Bereavement in Contemporary Society: Bridging Research and Practice*, eds. R. A. Neimeyer, H. Winokuer, G. F. Thornton, and D. Harris. New York: Routledge, 2011.

Harris, Darcy. "Oppression of the Bereaved: A Critical Analysis of Grief in Western Society." *OMEGA: Journal of Death and Dying* 60, no. 3 (2010), 241–53.

Harvard Health Publications. "Complicated Grief." December 2006. https://www.health.harvard.edu/family-health-guide/Complicated-grief.html.

Henderson, Artis. *Unremarried Widow.* New York: Simon & Schuster, 2014.

Jacobs, Selby C. *Traumatic Grief.* Philadelphia: Brunner/Mazel, 1999.

James, John W., and Russell Friedman. *The Grief Recovery Handbook.* New York: HarperCollins Publishers, 1998.

Jordan, John R., and Joanne L. Harpel. "Grief after Suicide: The Impact on Families." *ADEC Forum* (January 2014): 1–5.

Klass, Dennis, Phyllis R. Silverman, and Steven L. Nickman. *Continuing Bonds.* New York: Routledge, 1996.

Kübler-Ross, Elisabeth. *On Life after Death.* Berkeley: Celestial Arts, 1991.

Levang, Elizabeth. *When Men Grieve.* Minneapolis: Fairview Press, 1998.

Lichtenthal, Wendy G., Robert A. Neimeyer, Joseph M. Currier, Kailey Roberts, and Nancy Jordan. "Cause of Death and the Quest for Meaning after the Loss of a Child." *Death Studies* (2013): 311–42.

Lindemann, Erich. "Symptomatology and Management of Acute Grief." *American Journal of Psychiatry* (1944): 141–48.

Marx, Robert J., and Susan Wengerhoff Davidson. *Facing the Ultimate Loss: Coping with the Death of a Child.* Fredonia: Champion Press, Ltd., 2003.

Mitchell, Ellen, et al. *Beyond Tears.* New York: St. Martin's Griffin, 2009.

Murphy, Shirley. "Bereaved Parents' Experiences: Mass Casualties vs. Individual Deaths." *Violent Death and Loss* (2014): 9–10.

Murphy, Shirley A., L. Clark Johnson, and Janet Lohan. "Finding Meaning in a Child's Violent Death: A Five-Year Prospective Analysis of Parents' Personal Narratives and Empirical Data." *Death Studies* (2003): 381–404.

Parkes, Colin Murray. *Bereavement Studies of Grief in Adult Life.* Philadelphia: Taylor & Francis Inc., 2001.

Pearlman, Laurie Anne, Camille B. Wortman, Catherine A. Feuer, Christine H. Farber, and Therese A. Rando. "Sudden, Traumatic Death and Traumatic Bereavement." In *Treating Traumatic Bereavement: A Practitioner's Guide*, by Laurie Anne Pearlman, Camille B. Wortman, Catherine A. Feuer, Christine H. Farber, and Therese A. Rando, 3–17. New York: The Guilford Press, 2014.

Petrie, Ronald G. *Into the Cave: When Men Grieve.* Portland: One to Another, Inc., 2001.

Rando, Therese A. *How to Go on Living when Someone You Love Dies.* New York: Bantam Books, 1988.

——. *Parental Loss of a Child.* Champaign, IL: Research Press, 1986.

——. *Treatment of Complicated Mourning.* Champaign, IL: Research Press, 1993.

Raphael, Beverley. *The Anatomy of Bereavement.* Northvale: Jason Aronson Inc., 1983.

Rolls, Liz, and Mairi Harper. "The Impact of Practical Support on Parental Bereavement: Reflections from a Study Involving Parents Bereaved Through Military Death." *Death Studies* 40, no. 2 (2015), 88–101. doi:10.1080/07481187.2015.1068247.

Rubin, Simon S., and Mor Shechory-Stahl. "The Continuing Bonds of Bereaved Parents: A Ten-Year Follow-Up Study with the Two-Track Model of Bereavement." *OMEGA: Journal of Death and Dying* 66, no. 4 (2013), 365–84.

Sanders, Catherine M. *Grief: The Mourning After.* New York: John Wiley & Sons, Inc., 1999.

——. *How to Survive the Loss of a Child.* Rocklin: Prima Publishing, 1992.

——. *Surviving Grief & Learning to Live Again.* New York: John Wiley & Sons, Inc., 1992.

Schupp, Linda J. *Assessing and Treating Trauma and PTSD.* Eau Claire: Pesi, 2004.

——. *Grief: Normal, Complicated, Traumatic.* Eau Claire: Pesi, 2007.

Shear, M. Katherine. "Complicated Grief and Violent Death." *ADEC Forum* (April 2014): 14–15.

——. "Grief and Mourning Gone Awry: Pathway and Course of Complicated Grief." *Dialogues in Clinical Neuroscience* (2012): 119–28.

Sheeler, Jim. *Final Salute.* New York: The Penguin Press, 2008.

Smolin, Ann, and John Guinan. *Healing after the Suicide of a Loved One.* New York: Simon & Schuster, 1993.

Steen, Joanne M., and M. Regina Asaro. *Military Widow: A Survival Guide.* Annapolis, MD: Naval Institute Press, 2006.

Tedeschi, Richard G., and Lawrence G. Calhoun. *Helping Bereaved Parents.* New York: Brunner-Routledge, 2004.

Wolfelt, Alan D. *Healing Your Traumatized Heart: 100 Practical Ideas.* Fort Collins, CO: Companion Press, 2002.

——. *Understanding Grief: Helping Yourself Heal.* New York: Brunner-Routledge, 1992.

Worden, J. William. *Grief Counseling and Grief Therapy.* New York: Springer Publishing Company, 1991.